折り紙建築
世界遺産をつくろう!
ORIGAMIC ARCHITECTURE
Let's Make World Heritage Buildings

茶谷正洋
Masahiro CHATANI

中沢圭子
Keiko NAKAZAWA

彰国社

装丁/犬塚勝一

英訳/アムスタッツ　コミュニケーションズ
撮影/和木　通
作品製作協力/茶谷亞矢、兵頭喜代子、陸　邦子
作品分担/
　　茶谷正洋　1,3,5,7,10,16,17,20,23,24,25,26,27,30,32,33,35,36,39,40,42,43,44
　　中沢圭子　2,4,6,8,9,11,12,13,14,15,18,19,21,22,28,29,31,34,37,38,41,45

Binding: Shouichi Inuzuka
Translator: Brian Amstutz Communications
Photographer: Toru Waki
Model Design Assistance: Aya Chatani, Kiyoko Hyodo, Kuniko Kuga
Works by Masahiro CHATANI　1,3,5,7,10,16,17,20,23,24,25,26,27,30,32,33,35,36,39,40,42,43,44
Works by Keiko NAKAZAWA　2,4,6,8,9,11,12,13,14,15,18,19,21,22,28,29,31,34,37,38,41,45

ORIGAMIC ARCHITECTURE
Let's Make World Heritage Buildings
By Masahiro CHATANI and Keiko NAKAZAWA
Copyright © Masahiro CHATANI and Keiko NAKAZAWA
2005
Published by SHOKOKUSHA Publishing Company, Ltd.
　　　　　　25 Sakamachi, Shinjuku, Tokyo, Japan
Printed in Japan
ISBN4-395-27047-6 C3072

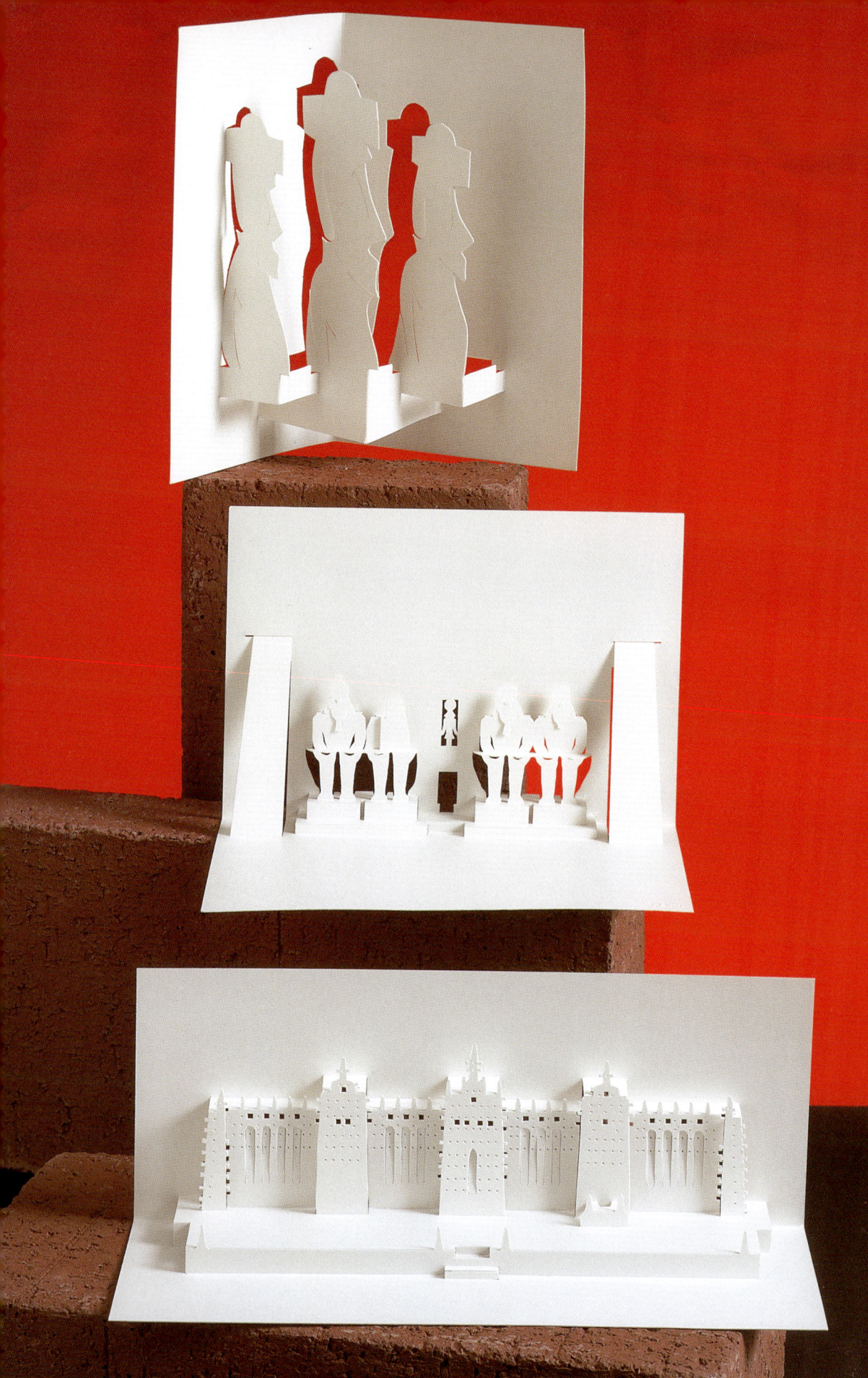

目次 Contents

口上　Preface —11
紙ワザ入門　用具と使用する紙　Getting Started in Origamic Architecture: Tools and Paper —13
90°作品の作り方　How to Create the 90°-angle Model —14
新90°作品の作り方　How to Create the New 90°-angle Model —15

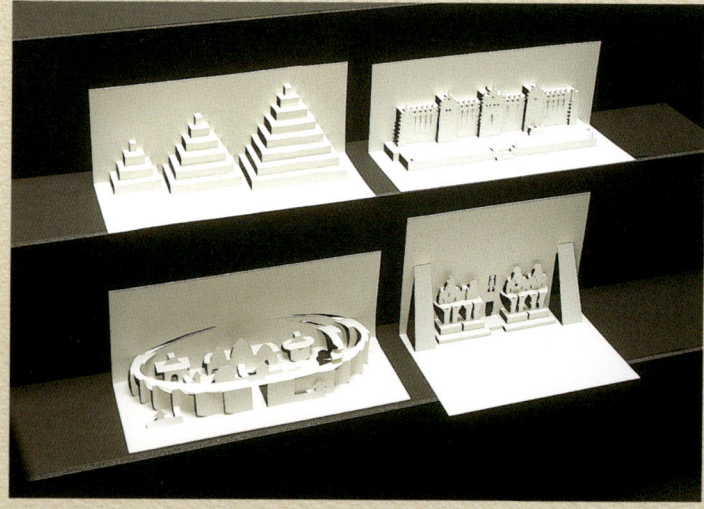

アフリカ Africa

1　ピラミッド —16
　　Pyramids (Egypt)

2　アブ・シンベル神殿 —17
　　Abu Simbel (Egypt)

3　グレート・ジンバブエ —18
　　Great Zimbabwe (Zimbabwe)

4　ジェンネの大モスク —19
　　Great Mosque of Djenné (Mali)

ヨーロッパ Europe

5 アルベロベッロのトゥルッリ —20
　Trulli of Alberobello (Italy)
6 サンタ・マリア・デル・フィオーレ大聖堂 —21
　Santa Maria del Fiore (Italy)
7 ヴィラ・ロトンダ —22
　Villa Rotonda (Italy)
8 ベレンの塔 —23
　Belém Tower (Portugal)
9 エッフェル塔 —24
　Eiffel Tower (France)
10 ノートル・ダム大聖堂 —25
　Notre-Dame Cathedral (France)
11 ウェストミンスター修道院 —26
　Westminster Abbey (United Kingdom)
12 アイアンブリッジ —27
　Ironbridge (United Kingdom)
13 ベルリンの博物館島・旧博物館 —28
　Altes Museum, Museum Island, Berlin (Germany)
14 リラ修道院 —30
　Rila Monastery (Bulgaria)

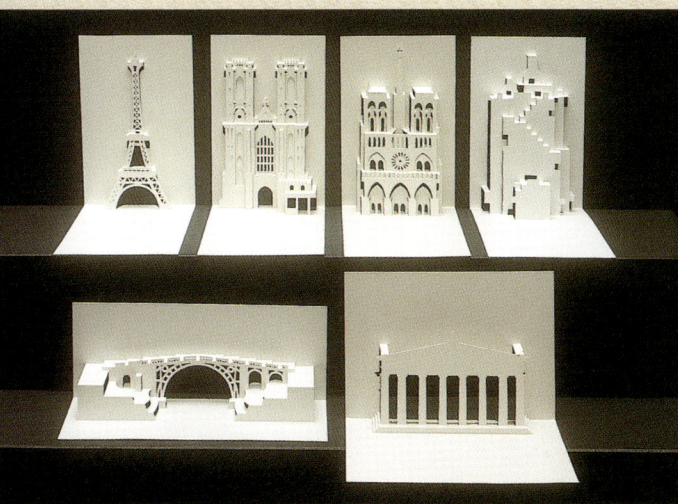

15 ザカリアス広場の家並み —32
　Square of Zachariás Renaissance Houses (Czech Republic)
16 パルテノン神殿 —33
　Parthenon (Greece)
17 メテオラの修道院 —34
　Meteora Monastery (Greece)
18 キジ島の木造教会 —35
　Transfiguration Church on Kizhi Island (Russia)

アジア Asia

19 アヤ・ソフィア —36
　Hagia Sofia (Turkey)
20 カッパドキアの洞窟聖堂 —37
　Cappadocia Church (Turkey)
21 ハトラ遺跡 —38
　Hatra (Iraq)
22 シバームの旧城壁都市 —39
　Old Walled City of Shibam (Yemen)
23 タージ・マハル —40
　Taj Mahal (India)
24 アンコール・ワット —41
　Angkor Wat (Cambodia)
25 ボロブドゥル寺院 —42
　Borobudur (Indonesia)
26 万里の長城 —43
　The Great Wall (China)
27 ポタラ宮 —44
　Potala Palace (China)
28 昌徳宮 —45
　Changdeok Palace (Republic of Korea)
29 宗廟 —46
　Chongmyo Shrine (Republic of Korea)

アジア Asia

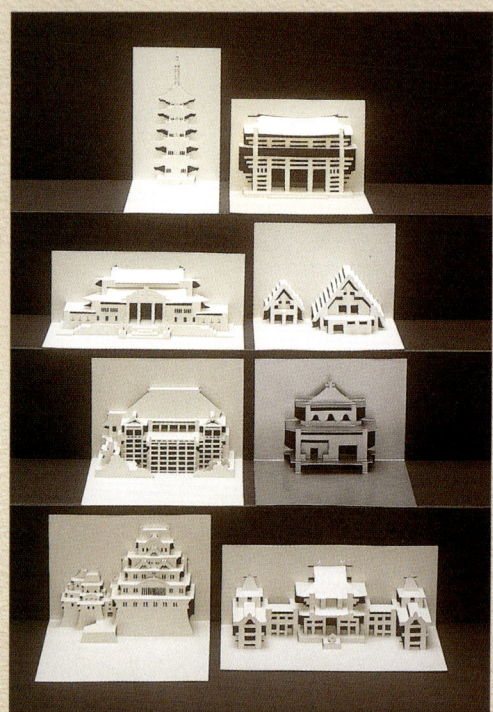

30 姫路城 —47
Himeji Castle (Japan)

31 清水寺 —48
Kiyomizu Temple (Japan)

32 銀閣寺 —49
Ginkakuji (Japan)

33 平等院鳳凰堂 —50
Phoenix Hall of Byodo-in (Japan)

34 東寺五重塔 —51
Toji Five-storied Pagoda (Japan)

35 東大寺南大門 —52
Todaiji Great South Gate (Japan)

36 合掌造り —53
Historic Villages of Shirakawa-go and Gokayama (Japan)

37 首里城 —54
Shuri Castle (Japan)

南北アメリカ North and South America

38 自由の女神像 —55
Statue of Liberty (United States)

39 タオス・プエブロ —56
Taos Pueblo (United States)

40 魔法使いのピラミッド —57
Pyramid of the Magician (Mexico)

41 ハバナ大聖堂 —58
Havana Cathedral (Cuba)

42 サン・ニコラス・デ・バリ病院 —59
San Nicolás de Bari Hospital (Dominican Republic)

43 マチュピチュ —60
Machu Picchu (Peru)

44 モアイ —61
Moais (Chile)

45 ブラジリアの国会議事堂 —62
Congress Building, Brasilia (Brazil)

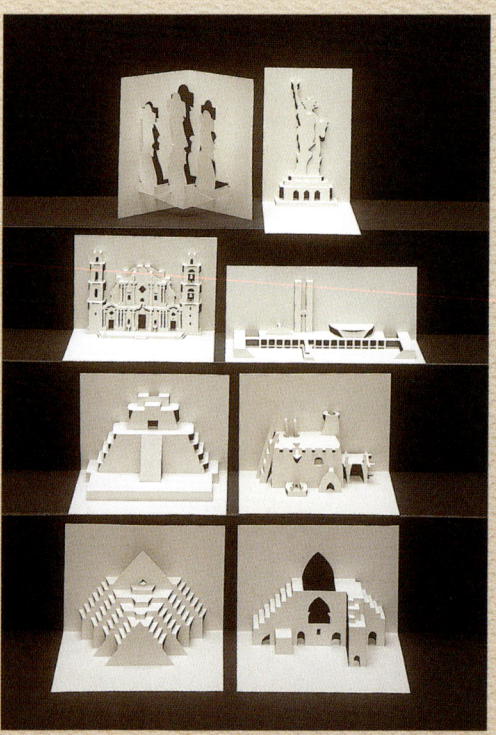

この本の世界遺産名・登録年　World Heritage Sites Appearing in This Book: Official Name and Year of Registration —63
あとがき　Postscript —67

口　　上

そもそもは大閑小忙の余技なりしを
知らずして世界のうちに広がりたる折り紙建築
この世の古今東西森羅万象摩訶不思議なるを
二つ折の紙に折り込みし20余年と生まれし愛好家
みな神ならぬ紙わざとて黒髪に霜の降るまで
かみわざ追うともまさに無限に至る事無し
これぞ世界に残されたる産物なり
折りし紙を建つればいつ何時も時空を旅すること限りなし
只今見参

　　2005年　秋　　　　　　　　　　　　　　創始家元謹白
　　　　　　　　　　　　　　　　　　　　　　茶谷正洋

Preface

Origamic Architecture—a simple hobby, it was,
for the long idle hours. It spread before I knew it
to nimble fingers the world over,
devotees from a score and more years of folding,
folding the wonders of all ages, all creation
into crisp paper. Not miracles of god, these,
but works of paper magic, pursued without end,
going nowhere, while my black hair
went white. But this—a product that will endure in the world!
To build with paper is to travel at your whim
without limits through time and space.
And here it is.

Masahiro Chatani
Originator, Origamic Architecture
Autumn 2005

紙ワザ入門　用具と使用する紙

Getting Started in Origamic Architecture : Tools and Paper

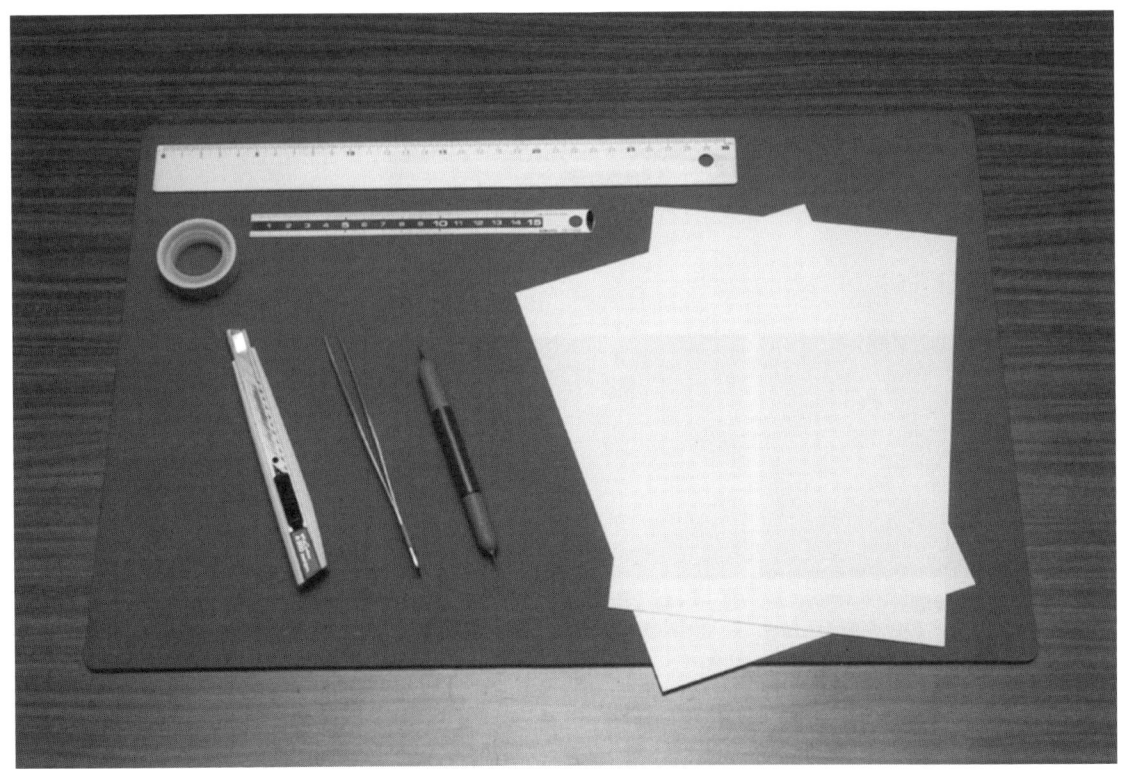

折り紙建築の製作には、用具と厚紙が必要です。
作品の型紙は、繰返し作ることができるよう、コピーして使うようにしましょう。

基本的な用具
カッターナイフ、ピンセット、鉄筆、定規、ドラフティングテープ、カッターマット

基本的な紙
白ケント紙（15×20 cm、10×30 cm）…厚手の紙で連量160〜180 kg くらいのもの

To make Origamic Architecture requires the tools below and stiff paper. Be sure to copy the pattern you want to use, so that the original pattern can be used again and again.

Basic Tools
Craft knife, tweezers, stylus (or needle), ruler, drafting tape, cutting mat

Basic Paper
White Kent (construction) paper (15×20cm, 10×30cm)...heavier weight paper of about 160-180 kg per 1,000 sheets (0.26mm thickness).

1 ピラミッド（エジプト）
Pyramids (Egypt)

ギザの三大ピラミッド。このごろは風化が激しく、登るのが難しくなったので、人工衛星で調べたりするそう。ピラミッドは究極の単純立体であり、その比類のないバランスが時空を超えて我々の心を捉える。

The three great Giza pyramids have weathered badly of late, making them difficult to climb. Satellites are therefore used in researching their deteriorating condition. The supreme simplicity and unrivaled balance of the pyramid's form have captured the human imagination throughout the ages.

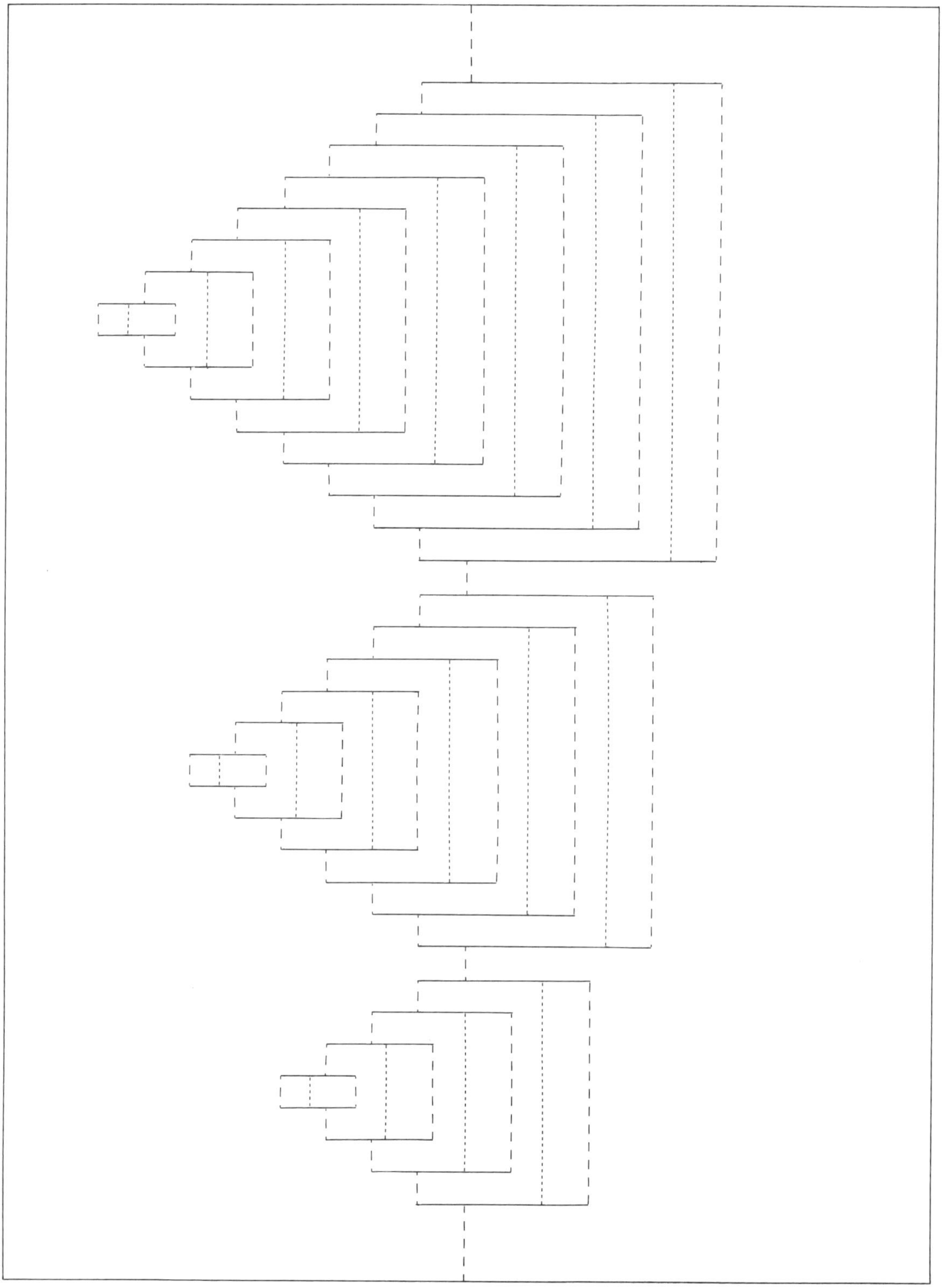

・・・・・・ 山折り線 Ridge fold line　― ― ― 谷折り線 Valley fold line　――― 切り線 Cutting line

2 アブ・シンベル神殿（エジプト）
Abu Simbel (Egypt)

紀元前1250年頃岩壁に穿たれたこの遺跡は、1960年代、アスワン・ハイ・ダムの建設に伴い水没の危機にさらされたが、ユネスコの呼びかけで地形ごと移築するという壮大な計画がなされ、1968年、古代と現代の共生が実現した。

These temples, carved from rock cliffs in BC 1250, were nearly submerged in the 1960's due to Aswan Dam construction. At UNESCO's behest, a giant project was undertaken to relocate the entire site, and in 1968 the ancient past attained coexistence with the present.

Africa

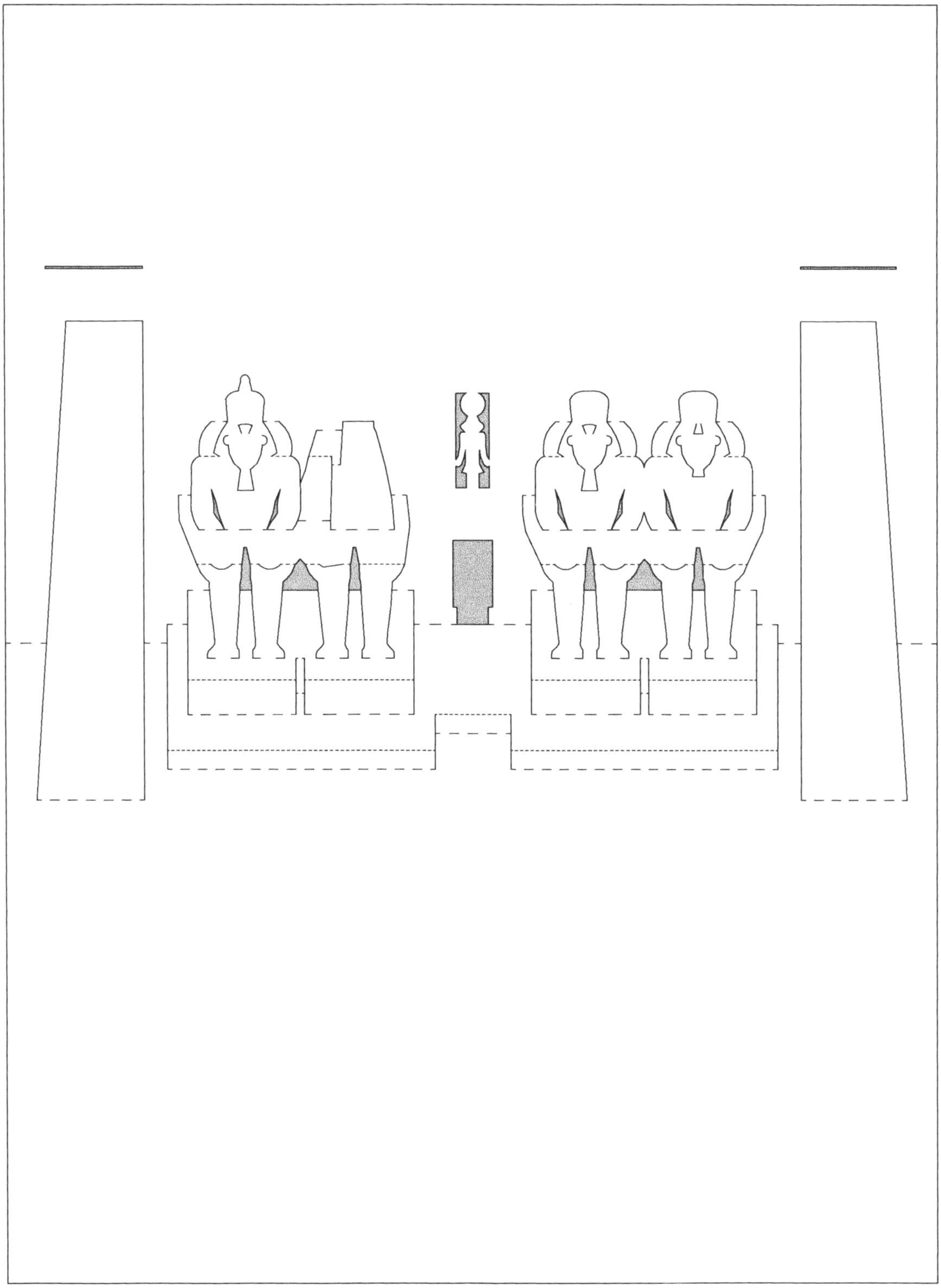

------ 山折り線 Ridge fold line　--- 谷折り線 Valley fold line　—— 切り線 Cutting line　▨ 切り落し Cutout

3　グレート・ジンバブエ（ジンバブエ）

Great Zimbabwe (Zimbabwe)

南部アフリカ最大の遺跡。ジンバブエとはショナ語で「石の家」の意味。遺跡は、丘の上の「アクロポリス」・高さ10ｍの石壁に囲まれた「神殿」・住居跡の「谷の遺跡」の3つの部分からなっている。

The name Zimbabwe derives from the Shona term for "great stone house." These ruins, the largest in Sub-Saharan Africa, consist of three distinct architectural groups: an acropolis on a hill, a shrine within 10m stone walls, and a valley complex of residences.

----- 山折り線 Ridge fold line　--- 谷折り線 Valley fold line　——— 切り線 Cutting line

4 ジェンネの大モスク (マリ)
Great Mosque of Djenné (Mali)

ジェンネは、サハラ砂漠南縁の古都トンブクトゥと内陸を結ぶ交易路の中継地。大モスクを取り囲む旧市街全体が世界遺産となっている。モスクの土壁は雨季に備え、毎年、周辺住民が一丸となって塗り替える。

Djenné was a trade center linking central Africa with the ancient West African city of Tombouctou. The entire old city around the Great Mosque is a registered World Heritage site. The Mosque's mud walls are annually re-coated by nearby residents ahead of the rainy season.

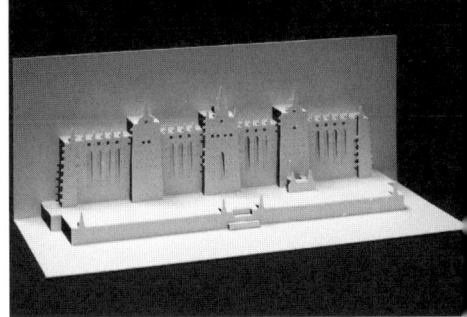

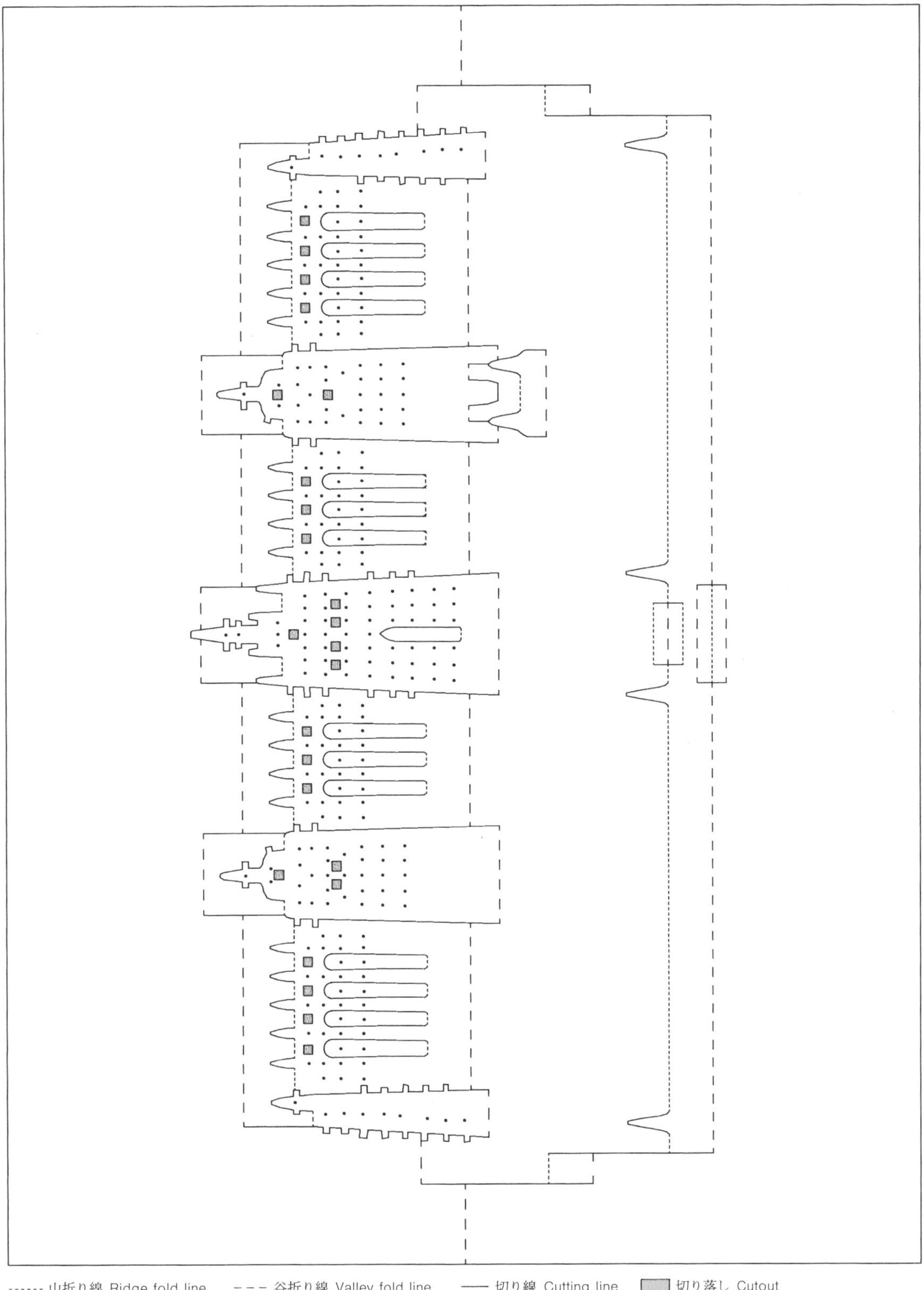

------ 山折り線 Ridge fold line   --- 谷折り線 Valley fold line   —— 切り線 Cutting line   ■ 切り落し Cutout

5 アルベロベッロのトゥルッリ（イタリア）
Trulli of Alberobello (Italy)

石造の民家トゥルッリ。「森の女神」という意味らしい。石灰岩を円錐形に積んだ屋根の住居群で、広場を挟む両側の斜面に波打つように連ねた住まい。このごろは、土産屋や民宿・食堂に改装されたものもあるとか。

"Trulli," a name perhaps meaning "forest goddess," have roofs of limestone rocks stacked in a conical form. These stone houses stand side by side, forming a wave-like procession up the slope, on either side of the square. Some now contain gift shops, inns, or restaurants.

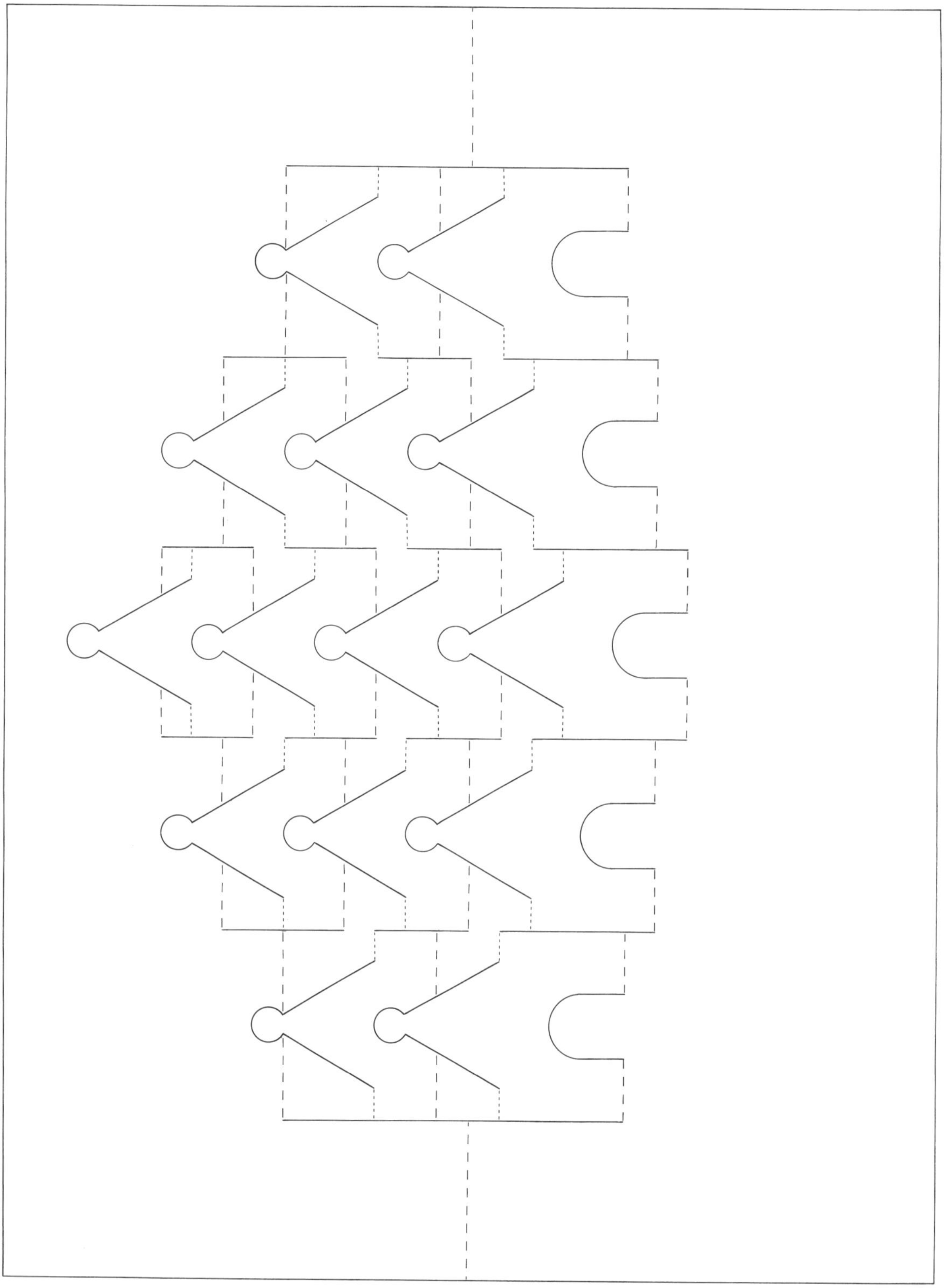

------ 山折り線 Ridge fold line　　--- 谷折り線 Valley fold line　　—— 切り線 Cutting line

6 サンタ・マリア・デル・フィオーレ大聖堂 (イタリア)
Santa Maria del Fiore (Italy)

ゴシック様式の聖堂に、巨大で美しいドーム屋根が完成したのは15世紀半ば。技術的な問題を解決しつつ、内部と外部のバランスを考えた新しい形が実現。外見の美しさを重んじたルネサンスの精神は、ここフィレンツェに始まった。

An enormous, beautiful dome was completed on this Gothic cathedral in the mid-15th century. By overcoming technical limitations, a new overall building of balanced interior and exterior was achieved. Thus the Renaissance spirit, which valued exterior beauty, was born in Florence.

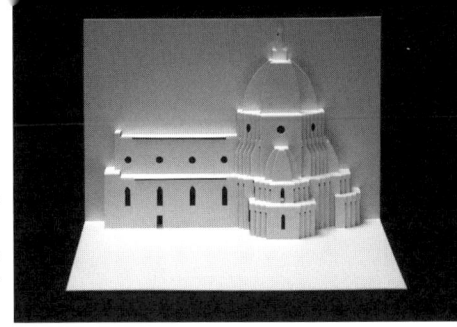

------ 山折り線 Ridge fold line　　--- 谷折り線 Valley fold line　　—— 切り線 Cutting line　　▨ 切り落し Cutout

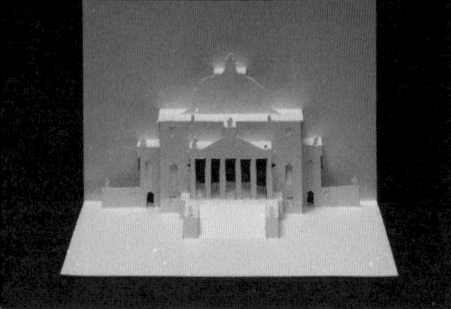

7 ヴィラ・ロトンダ（イタリア）
Villa Rotonda (Italy)

ルネサンス後期の建築家アンドレア・パラーディオは、世界で初めて自分の設計図を作品集(『建築四書』)に作り、パラディアンスタイルを広めた人。英国王立建築家協会別館に通って、その和紙にも似た400年前の図面の鉛筆のタッチに感激。

The late-Renaissance architect Andrea Palladio, creator of the Palladian style, was the world's first to compile his designs in a publication: *The Four Books on Architecture*. At annex to the Royal Institute of British Architects I savored his sensitive line on what looks like Japanese paper, in these 400-year-old drawings.

Europe

------ 山折り線 Ridge fold line   --- 谷折り線 Valley fold line   ——— 切り線 Cutting line

8 ベレンの塔（ポルトガル）
Belém Tower (Portugal)

海洋王国ポルトガルの基礎を築いたエンリケ王子と、インド航路の開拓者であるヴァスコ・ダ・ガマの偉業を称えて建立された、ジェロニモス修道院とベレンの塔は、東西貿易で繁栄の極みにあった、ポルトガル黄金時代の優美な記念碑。

Jerónimos Monastery and Belém Tower commemorate the achievements of Henry the Navigator, who established Portugal as a major sea power, and Vasco da Gama, who discovered a sea route to India. They are elegant monuments to Portugal's glory years of power and wealth.

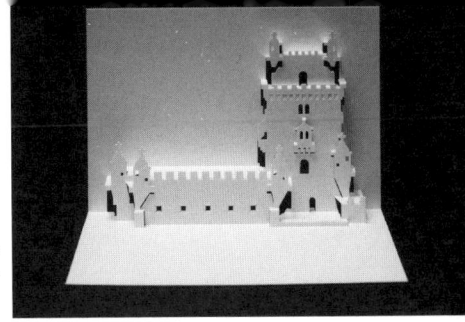

------ 山折り線 Ridge fold line　　--- 谷折り線 Valley fold line　　—— 切り線 Cutting line　　▨ 切り落し Cutout

9　エッフェル塔（フランス）
Eiffel Tower (France)

パリのセーヌ河岸に立つエッフェル塔は、末広がりの4本の脚だけで支えられる巨大な鉄の塔。「鉄のレース細工」とも称される細い鉄骨の幾何学的な組合せや、塔の真下が広場となって抜けている構成が、マクロで見た美しさを創り出している。

Only four broadening legs support this colossal tower standing near the Seine River in Paris. The beauty of its silhouette derives from its delicate, geometric steel assemblies, known as "iron lace," and its open base with space for a plaza.

15 cm

······　山折り線　Ridge fold line
— — —　谷折り線　Valley fold line
─────　切り線　Cutting line
▓▓▓▓　切り落し　Cutout

10 ノートル・ダム大聖堂 (フランス)
Notre-Dame Cathedral (France)

パリに行くと必ず、このローズウィンドウのステンドグラスに会いに行く。他と同様、この教会も狭い階段を上って屋上に出ると、間近に細部の彫刻や石工の細工が見られ、遙かに街を望む景色を眺められる。最も美しいゴシック聖堂。

Whenever in Paris, I go to see the stained glass of Notre-Dame's rose windows. As in other cathedrals, one can climb a narrow stairway to the roof to admire its sculptures and stonemasonry while enjoying panoramic city views. The most beautiful Gothic cathedral.

15 cm

------ 山折り線 Ridge fold line
--- 谷折り線 Valley fold line
—— 切り線 Cutting line
▨ 切り落し Cutout

Europe

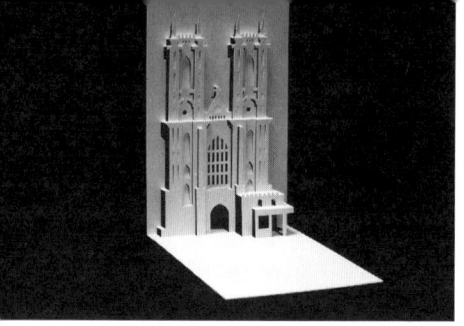

11　ウェストミンスター修道院 (イギリス)
Westminster Abbey (United Kingdom)

修道院は、テムズ河畔のウェストミンスター地区に建つイギリス国会議事堂や、セント・マーガレット教会と隣接して建つ。歴代国王の戴冠式が行われる場として有名。

This abbey church, standing near the Houses of Parliament and Saint Margaret's Church in Westminster, a district on the Thames River, is famous as a place of coronation for English monarchs.

15 cm

------　山折り線 Ridge fold line
- - -　谷折り線 Valley fold line
―――　切り線 Cutting line
▮　切り落し Cutout

12 アイアンブリッジ（イギリス）
Ironbridge (United Kingdom)

アイアンブリッジは1779年の産業革命期、バーミンガムの西、セヴァーン川渓谷に架けられた世界最古の鉄橋。鉄の時代の幕開けの地として「アイアンブリッジ渓谷」の名で登録された。

The world's oldest cast-iron bridge, Ironbridge was built across the Severn River Gorge, west of Birmingham, in 1779 during the industrial revolution. The region is registered under the name "Ironbridge Gorge" as the cradle of the steel age.

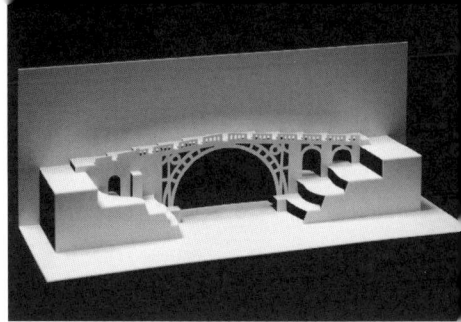

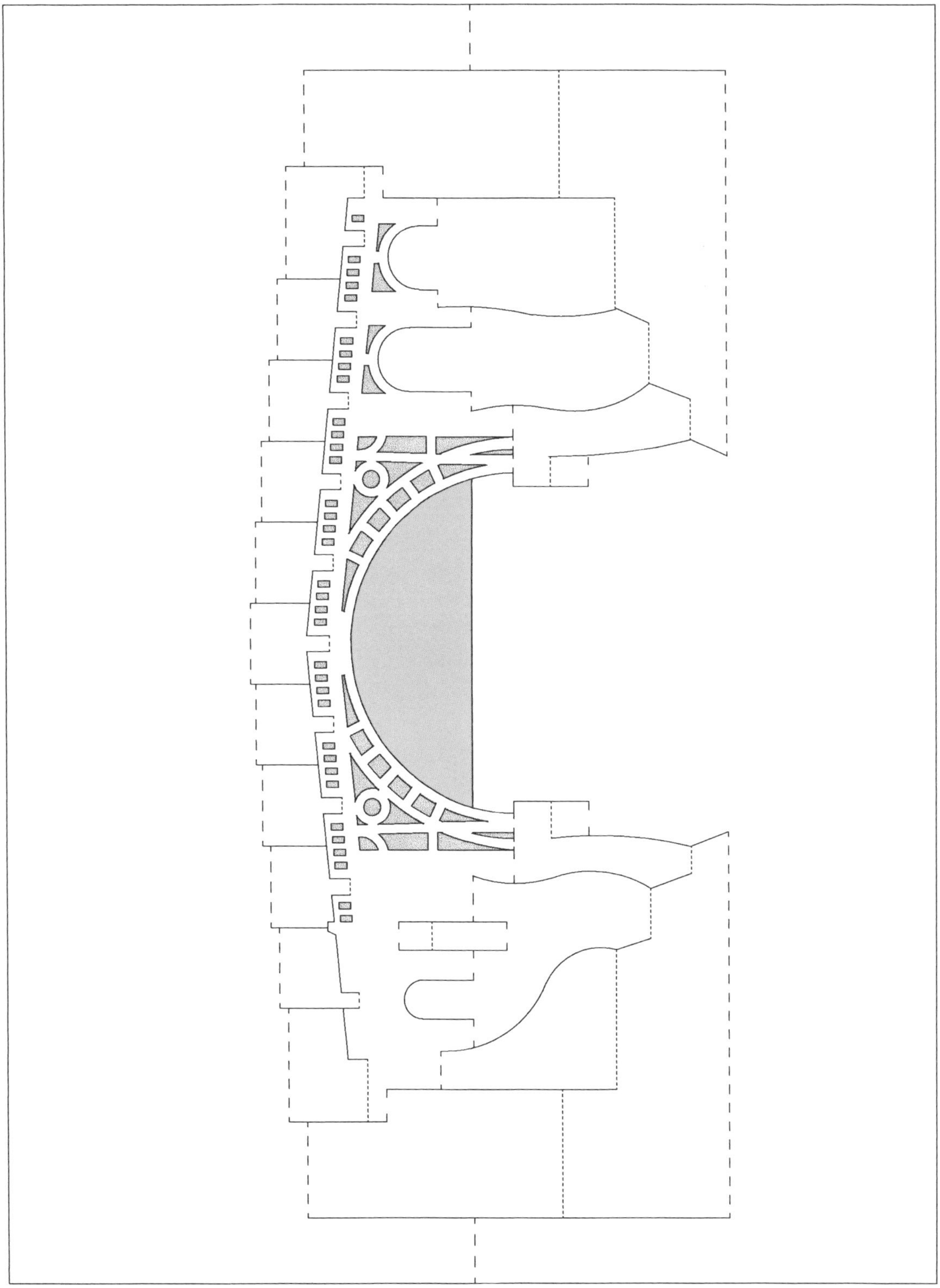

----- 山折り線 Ridge fold line　--- 谷折り線 Valley fold line　―― 切り線 Cutting line　■ 切り落し Cutout

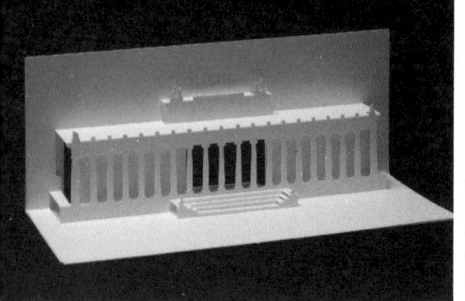

13 ベルリンの博物館島・旧博物館（ドイツ）
Altes Museum, Museum Island, Berlin (Germany)

旧博物館は、19世紀のドイツを代表する建築家シンケルの作で、最も美しい新古典主義の博物館建築として称えられた。島に架かるシュロス橋の傍らにはシンケルの像が立ち、東西統一後の修復で甦った博物館を見守り続ける。

The Altes Museum, designed by 19th century German architect Karl Friedrich Schinkel, is considered the finest museum in the neoclassic style. A statue of Schinkel beside Schlossbrücke Bridge watches over the Museum, which was renovated after Germany's reunification.

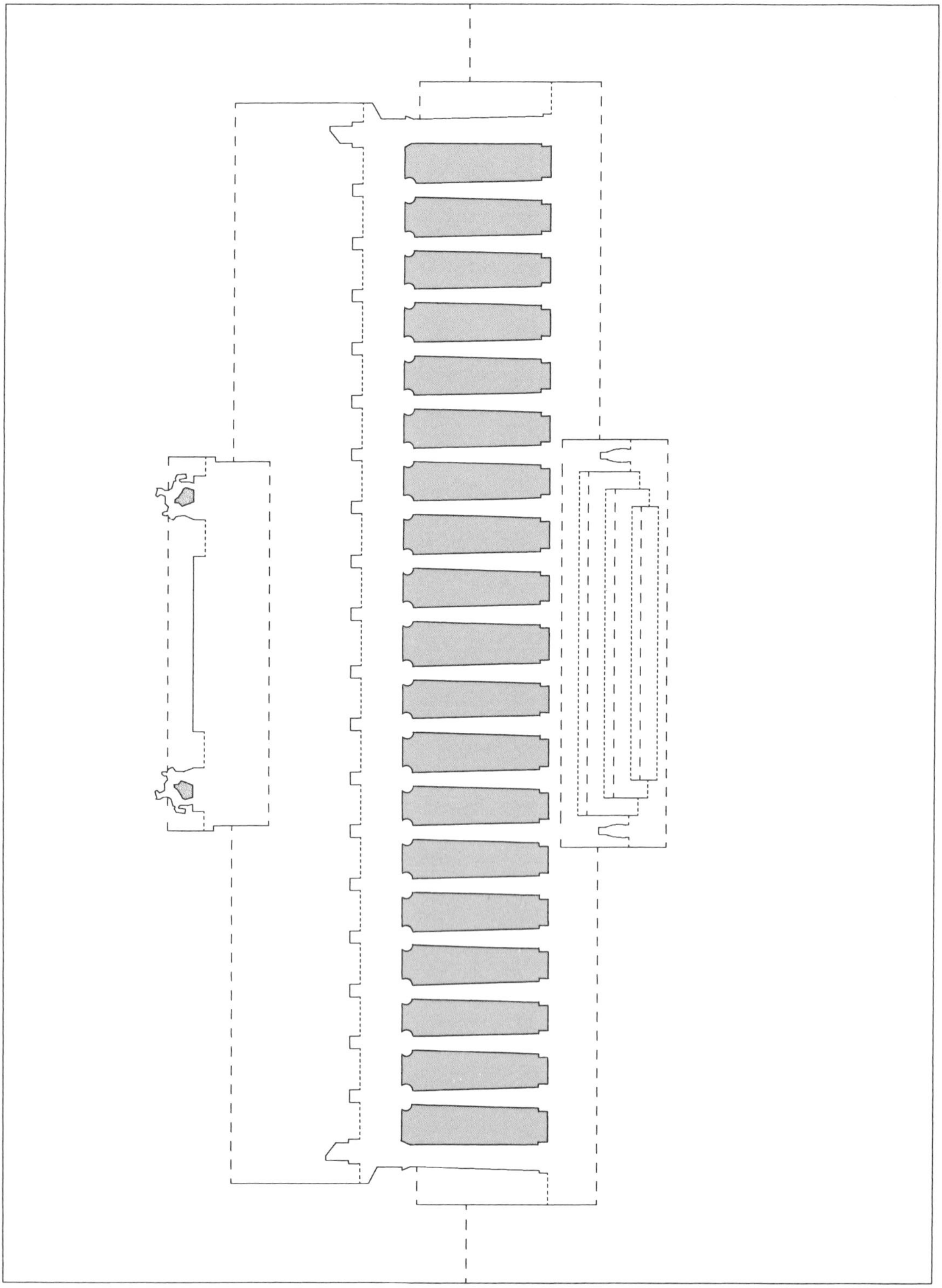

[型図 A]

・・・・・・ 山折り線 Ridge fold line　　--- 谷折り線 Valley fold line　　―― 切り線 Cutting line　　▨ 切り落し Cutout

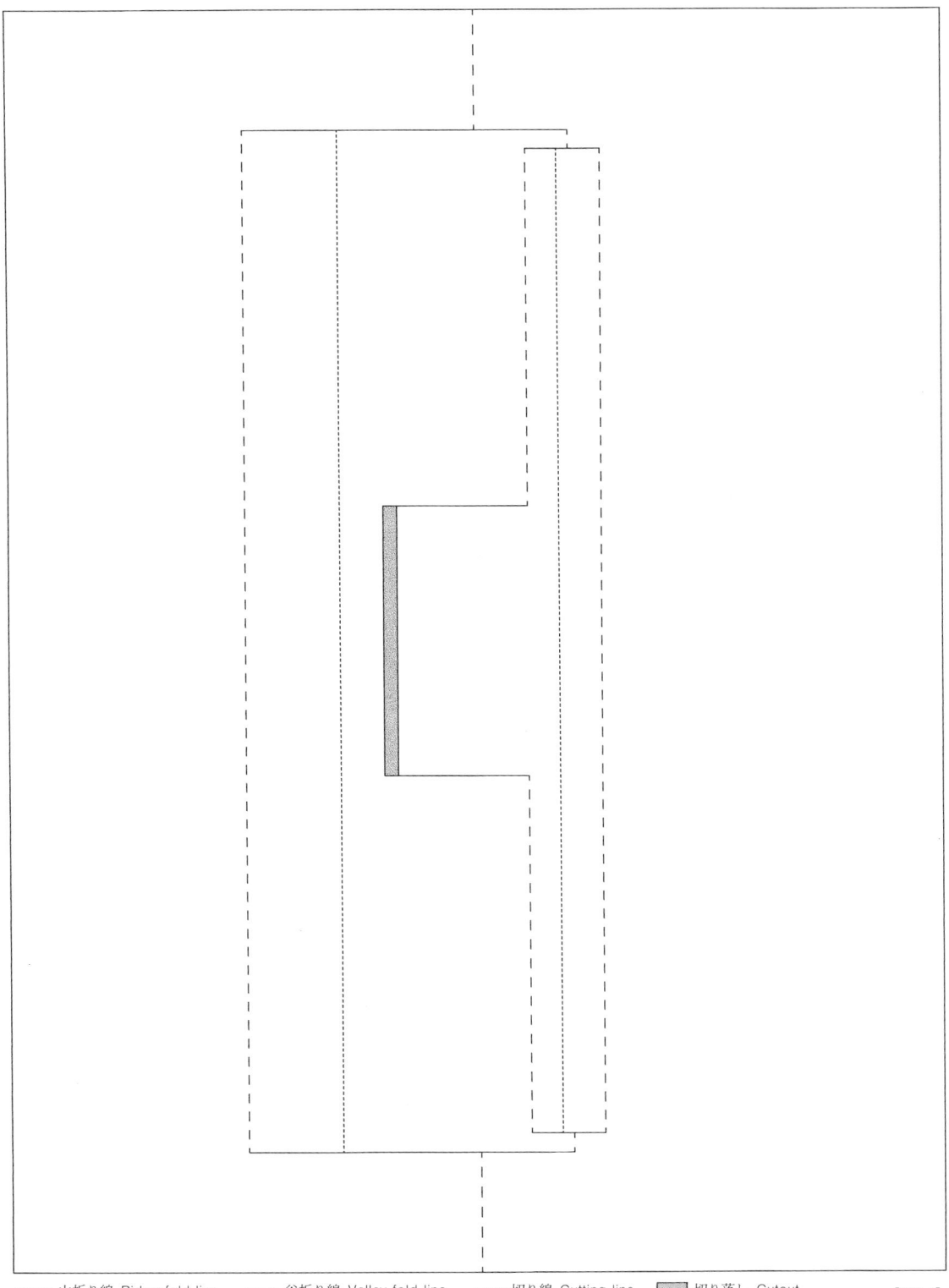

------ 山折り線 Ridge fold line   --- 谷折り線 Valley fold line   —— 切り線 Cutting line   ▓ 切り落し Cutout

[型図B]

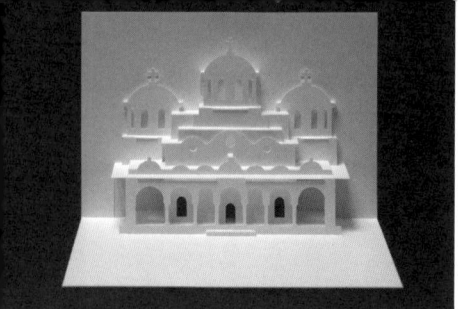

14 リラ修道院（ブルガリア）
Rila Monastery (Bulgaria)

首都のソフィアから南に約 120 km、標高 1,147 m のリラの山中にあるリラ修道院は、ブルガリア正教の総本山。500 年にも及ぶオスマン・トルコの支配など、数々の苦難を乗り越えて復興したブルガリアの精神的支柱となっている。

This monastery, the head temple of Bulgaria's Orthodox Church, stands on 1,147m Rila Mountain, about 120km south of Sofia, the capital. Today, it symbolizes the enduring spirit of the Bulgarians, who have surmounted tremendous hardship, including 500 years of occupation by the Ottoman Empire.

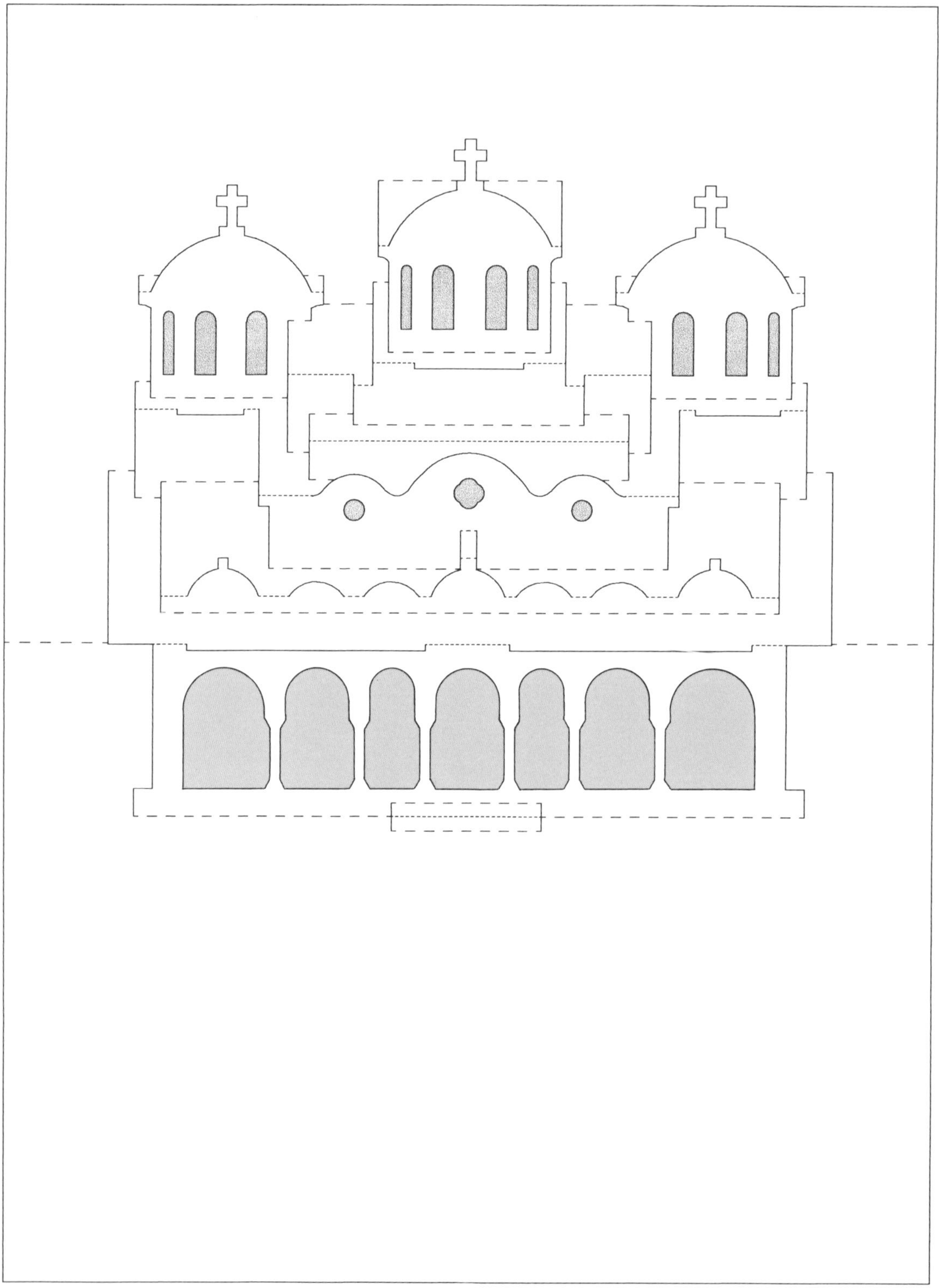

[型図 A]

------ 山折り線 Ridge fold line　　− − − 谷折り線 Valley fold line　　──── 切り線 Cutting line　　▨ 切り落し Cutout

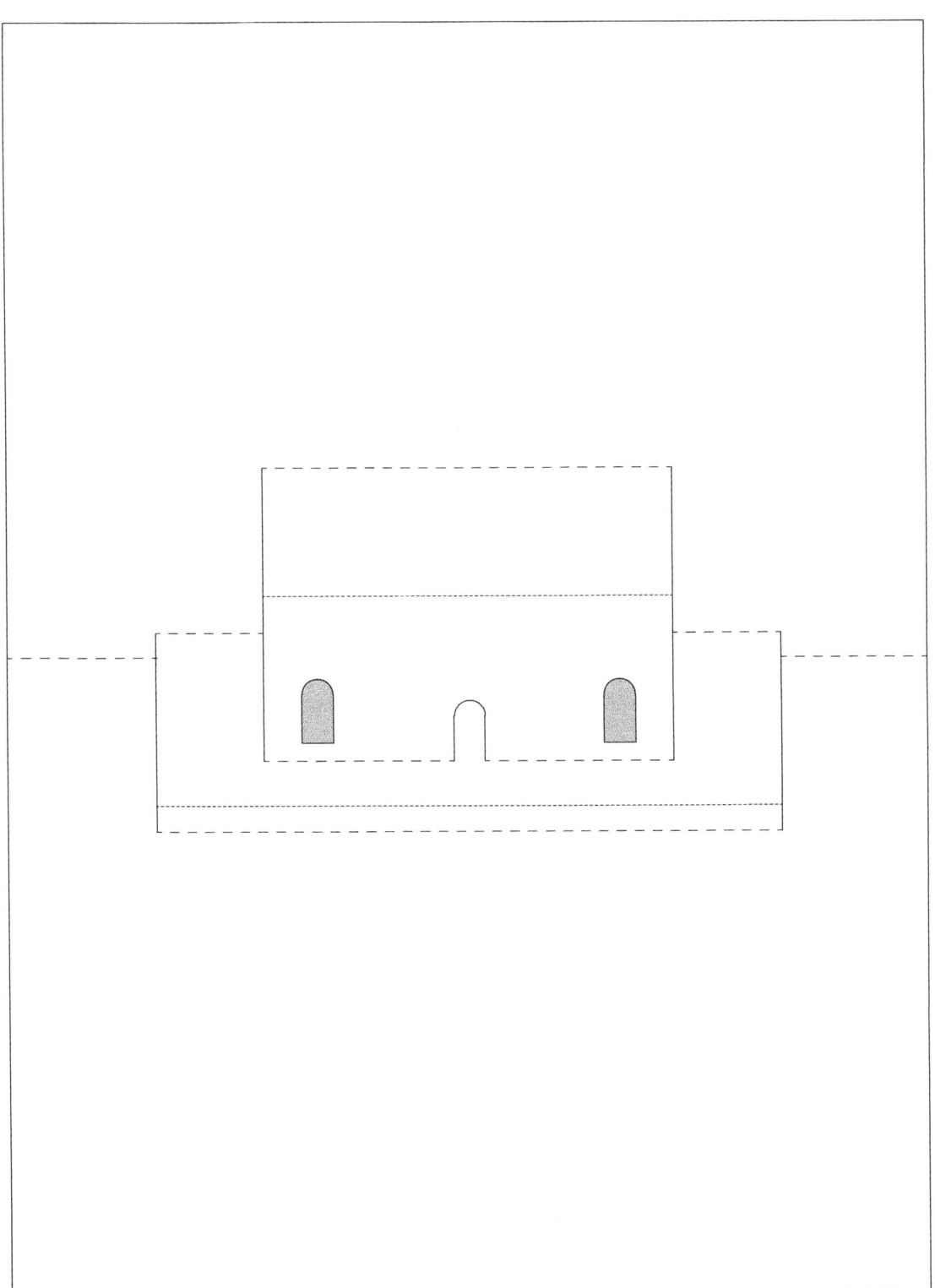

------ 山折り線 Ridge fold line   --- 谷折り線 Valley fold line   —— 切り線 Cutting line   ▨ 切り落し Cutout

Europe

[型図B]

15　ザカリアス広場の家並み（チェコ）
Square of Zachariás Renaissance Houses (Czech Republic)

南ボヘミア地方の小さな町テルチは、1530年の大火で焦土と化したが、復興にあたり、広場に面するすべての建物は、ルネサンス様式と初期バロック様式によること、という市長の通達のもとに再建された。

The small town of Telc in the southern Bohemia region was destroyed by fire in 1530. In reconstructing, the mayor had all the buildings facing on the square rebuilt in the Renaissance and early Baroque styles.

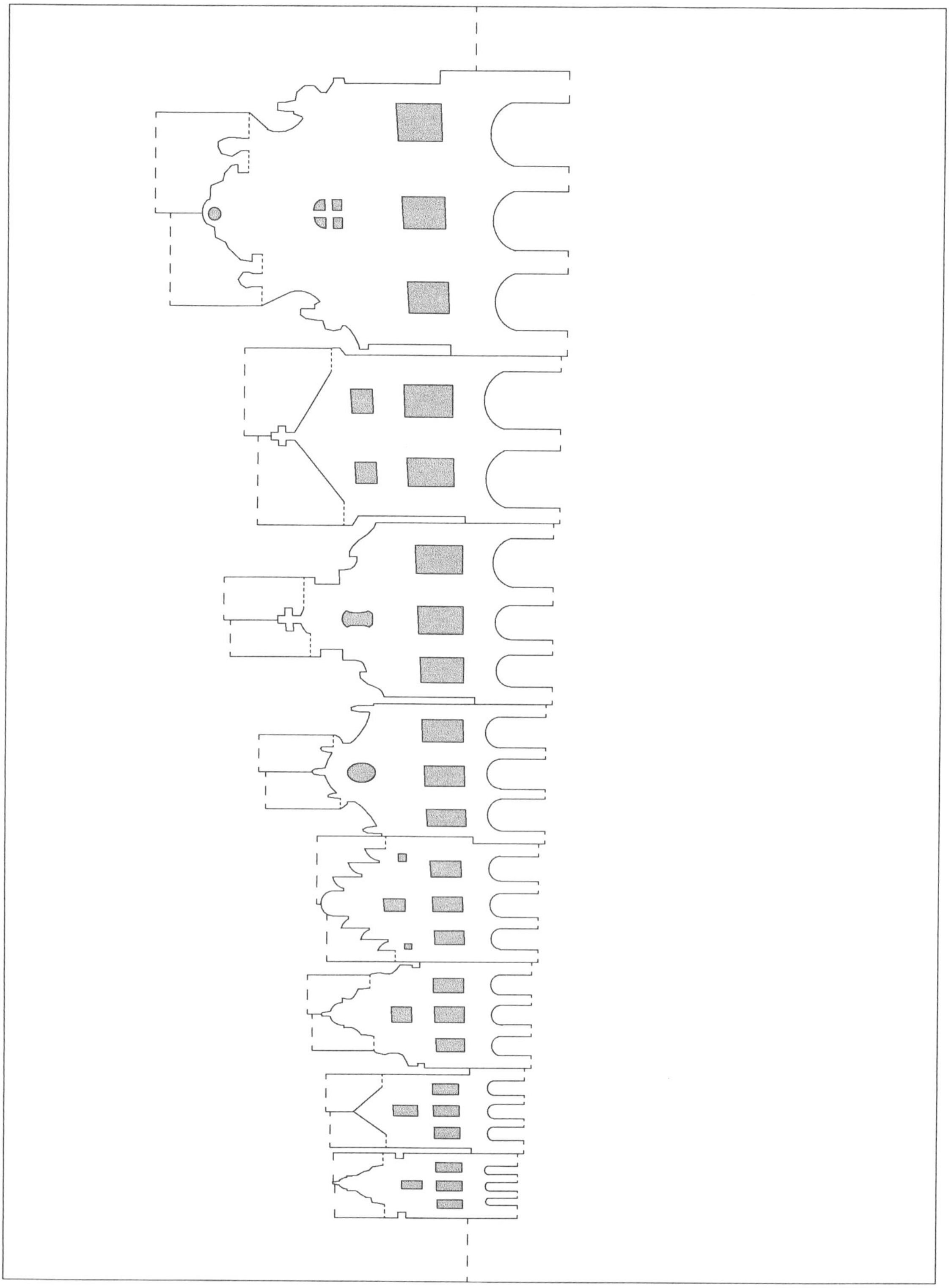

------ 山折り線 Ridge fold line　--- 谷折り線 Valley fold line　—— 切り線 Cutting line　▨ 切り落し Cutout

16 パルテノン神殿（ギリシア）
Parthenon (Greece)

アテネの中心にあるアクロポリスの丘に建つ、最高に美しい神殿。今は手すりがついて近づけないが、昔は誰でも柱や中の大理石に触れ、一日中座り込んで、夕方になるとともにピンク色に染まるまで眺めていられた。

A temple of paramount beauty, standing atop the Acropolis in central Athens. Hand rails keep viewers at a distance, these days, but formerly one could touch its pillars and marble interior and sit all day gazing until it turned rosy pink in the setting sun.

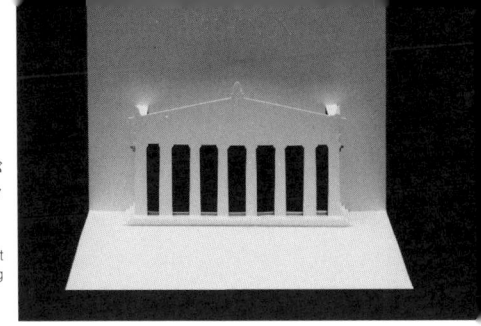

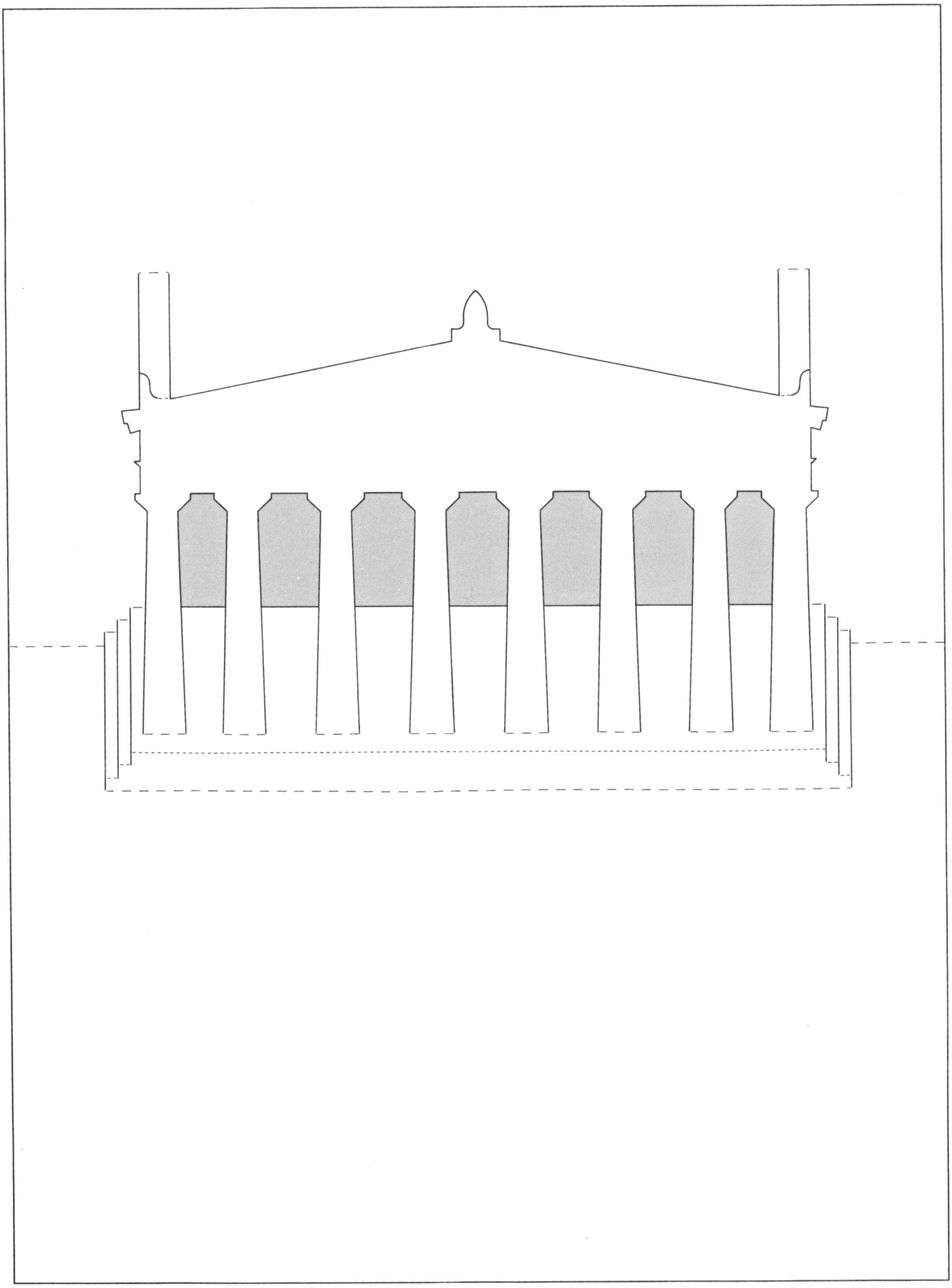

------ 山折り線 Ridge fold line   - - - 谷折り線 Valley fold line   —— 切り線 Cutting line   ▨ 切り落し Cutout

17　メテオラの修道院（ギリシア）
Meteora Monastery (Greece)

9世紀のキリスト教弾圧の状況下、神に近い場所として岩の頂に建てた庵が始まり。地上とは縄梯子で往来していた。

Meteora was founded as a hermitage, high atop a cliff close to god, during times of Christian persecution in the 9th century. From the ground, it could only be reached using rope ladders.

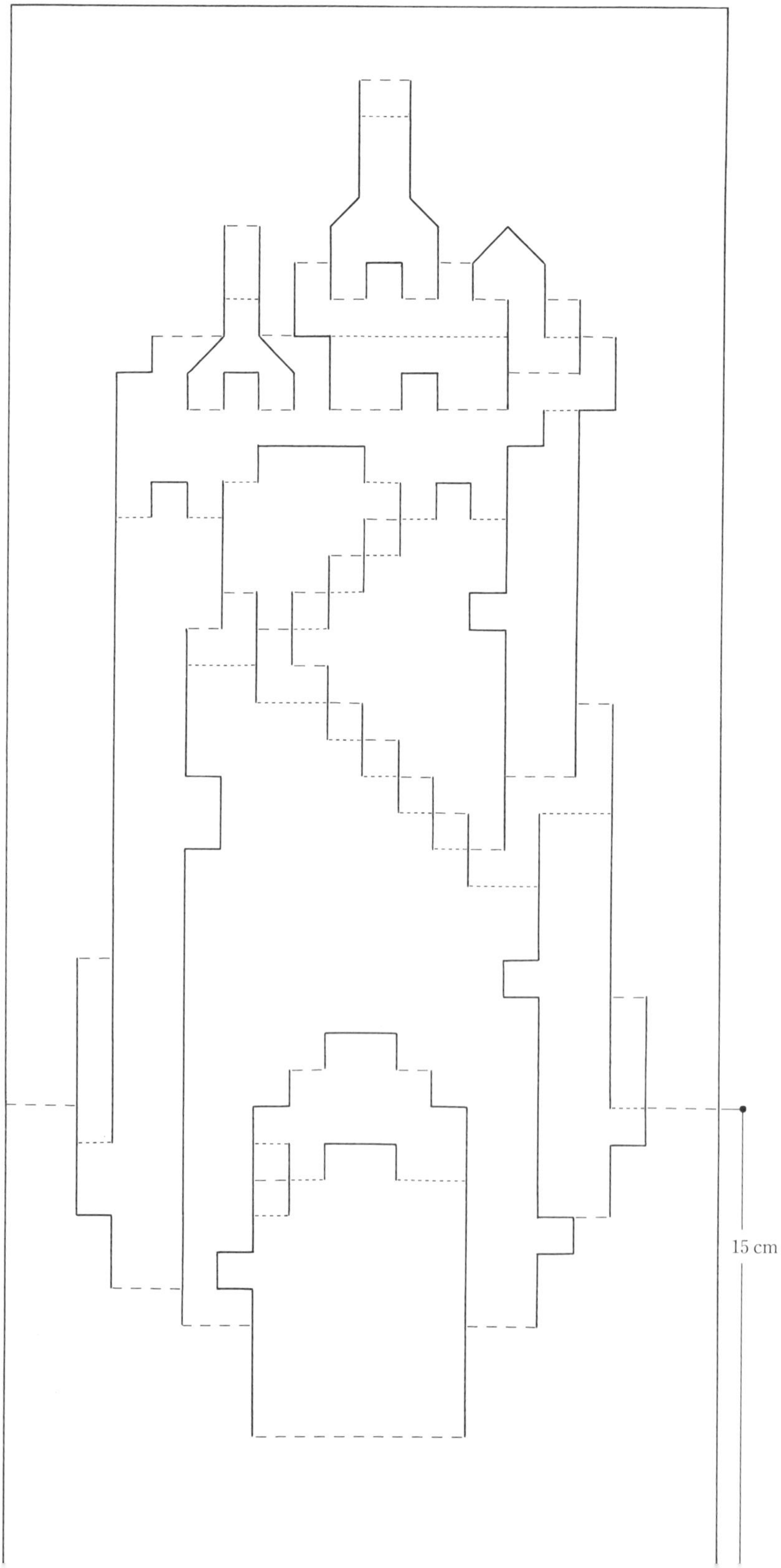

Europe

15 cm

...... 山折り線 Ridge fold line
--- 谷折り線 Valley fold line
——— 切り線 Cutting line

18　キジ島の木造教会（ロシア）

Transfiguration Church on Kizhi Island (Russia)

サンクト・ペテルブルグ（旧レニングラート）の北東約300kmの、オネガ湖に浮かぶキジ島は、ロシア伝統の木造建築の野外博物館。なかでも玉葱型ドームが重なる幻想的な木造教会は、伝統を継承してきた職人技の賜物。

Kizhi Island in Onego lake, about 300km northeast of Saint Petersburg (formerly Leningrad) is an open-air museum of Russian traditional wooden buildings. Among them, the phantasmal Transfiguration Church, with its onion-shaped domes, is a legacy of traditional craftsman skills.

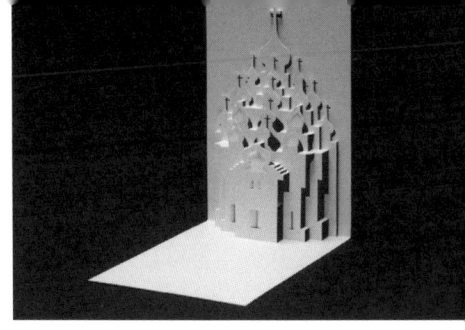

Europe

15 cm

------　山折り線　Ridge fold line
- - -　谷折り線　Valley fold line
———　切り線　Cutting line
▨　切り落し　Cutout

19 アヤ・ソフィア（トルコ）
Hagia Sofia (Turkey)

イスタンブールの歴史地区に建つアヤ・ソフィアは、神を意味する「聖なる・叡智」に捧げられた聖堂。建立は360年とされるが、現在のアヤ・ソフィアは537年に建てられたビザンティン建築の最高傑作。

Hagia Sofia, located in Istanbul's historical district, was first constructed as a temple devoted to Hagia (Saint) Sofia in 360, it is thought. The present building, a masterpiece of Byzantine architecture, dates from 537.

----- 山折り線 Ridge fold line　--- 谷折り線 Valley fold line　—— 切り線 Cutting line　▨ 切り落し Cutout

20　カッパドキアの洞窟聖堂（トルコ）
Cappadocia Church (Turkey)

300万年前に火山の噴火で大量の火山灰を浴びた際に堆積された凝灰岩窟が、湧き水や雨などで長い年月をかけて浸食され、珍岩奇岩が林立する独特の風景を生み出した。でも本当に驚くべきは、この地下に、実は一大都市が築かれていたことである。

Caves formed by layered volcanic ash accumulating during eruptions three million years ago were eroded by springwater and rain over great time, producing a scenery of bizarre rock figures. Even more astonishing, however, is the great city that was carved underground, below them.

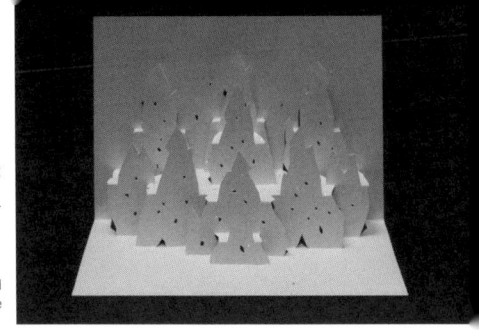

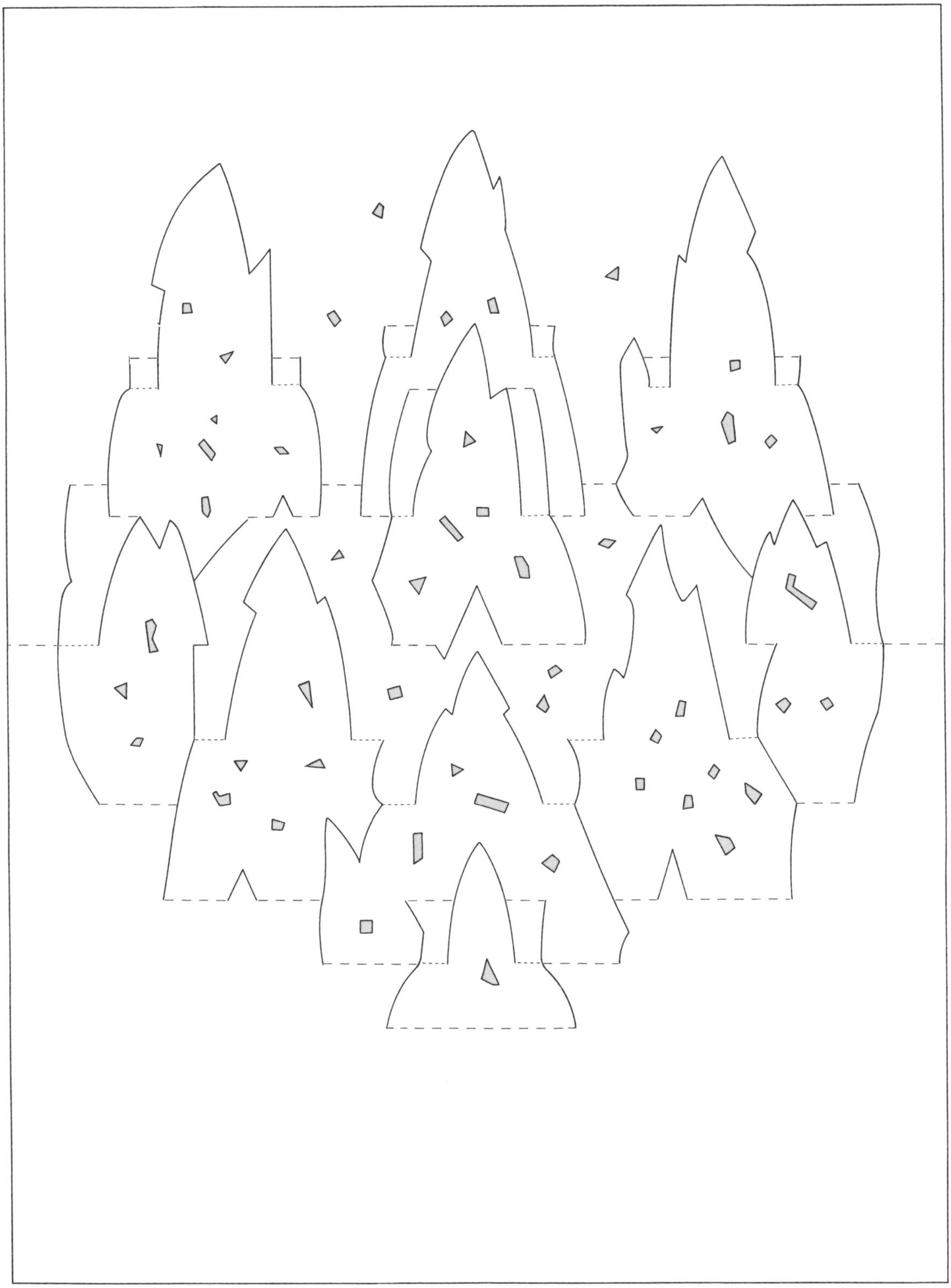

------　山折り線 Ridge fold line　　- - -　谷折り線 Valley fold line　　―――　切り線 Cutting line　　▨　切り落し Cutout

Asia

37

21 ハトラ遺跡（イラク）
Hatra (Iraq)

ハトラは、イラク北部にあるパルティア時代の都市遺跡。シルクロードの隊商都市として発展したが、ローマ帝国と戦う軍事拠点としても栄えてきた。
Hatra is the ruins of a Parthian-age city located in northern Iraq. Hatra developed as a caravan post on the Silk Road and later flourished as a military base for conducting wars with the Roman Empire.

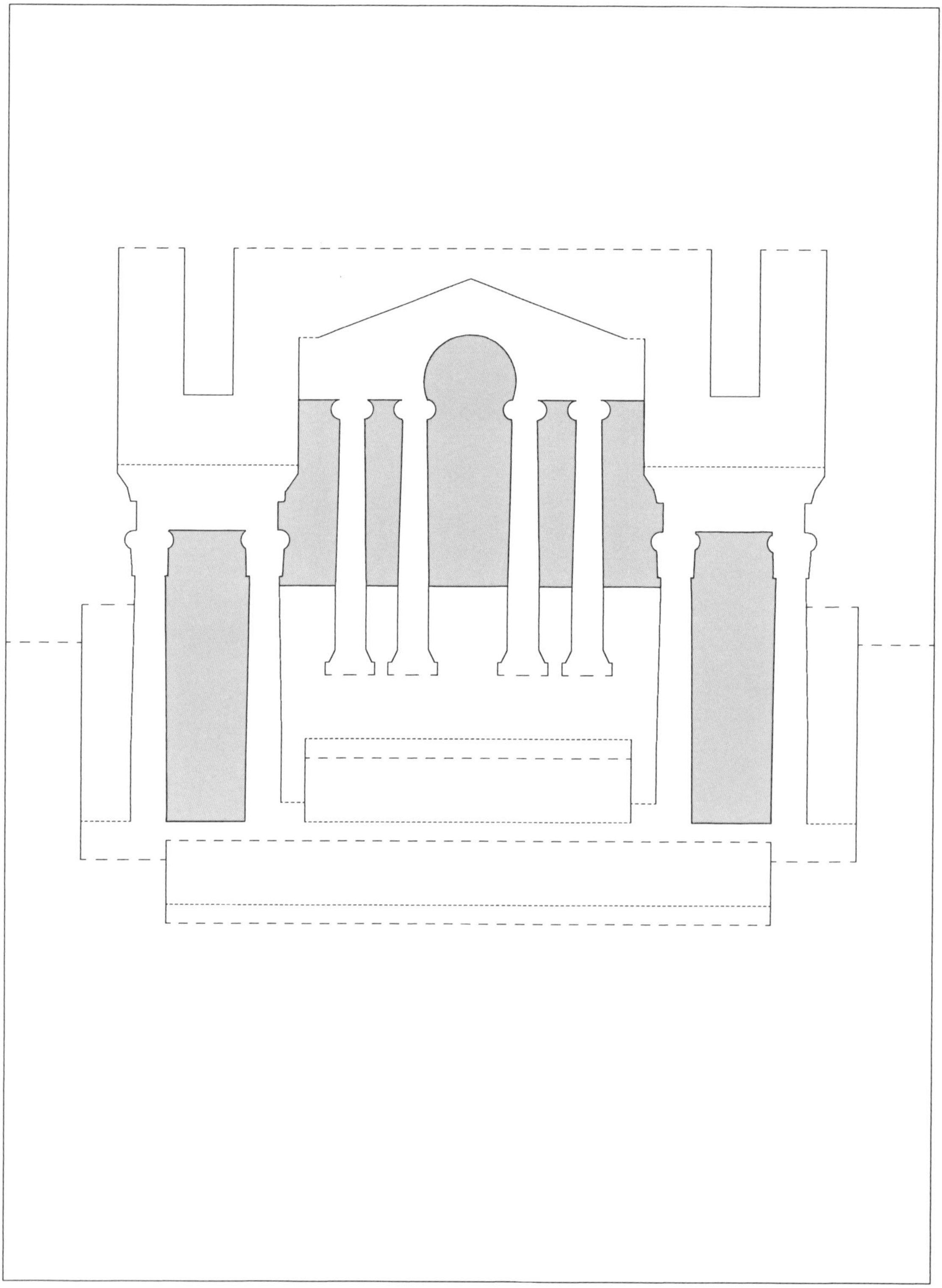

------ 山折り線 Ridge fold line   - - - 谷折り線 Valley fold line   —— 切り線 Cutting line   切り落し Cutout

22 シバームの旧城壁都市（イエメン）
Old Walled City of Shibam (Yemen)

イエメン中部ハドラマウト州のシバームは、3世紀頃からこの地方で栄えた町。城壁で囲まれた旧市街には、約500棟の土壁の高層家屋が建ち並び、その多くが築100年前後のものだという。遠望はさながら「砂漠のマンハッタン」。

Shibam, in Hadramawt province in central Yemen, flourished from about the 3rd century. Some 500 tower houses of mud brick stand in its walled historic quarter, many thought to be around 100 years old. Shibam's appearance has earned it the name, "Manhattan of the desert."

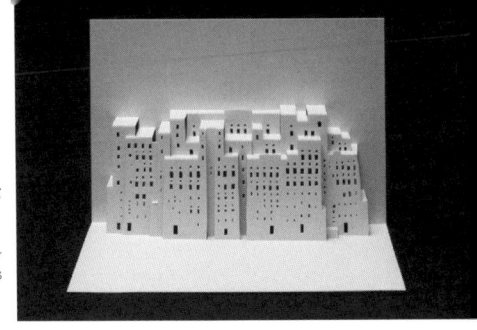

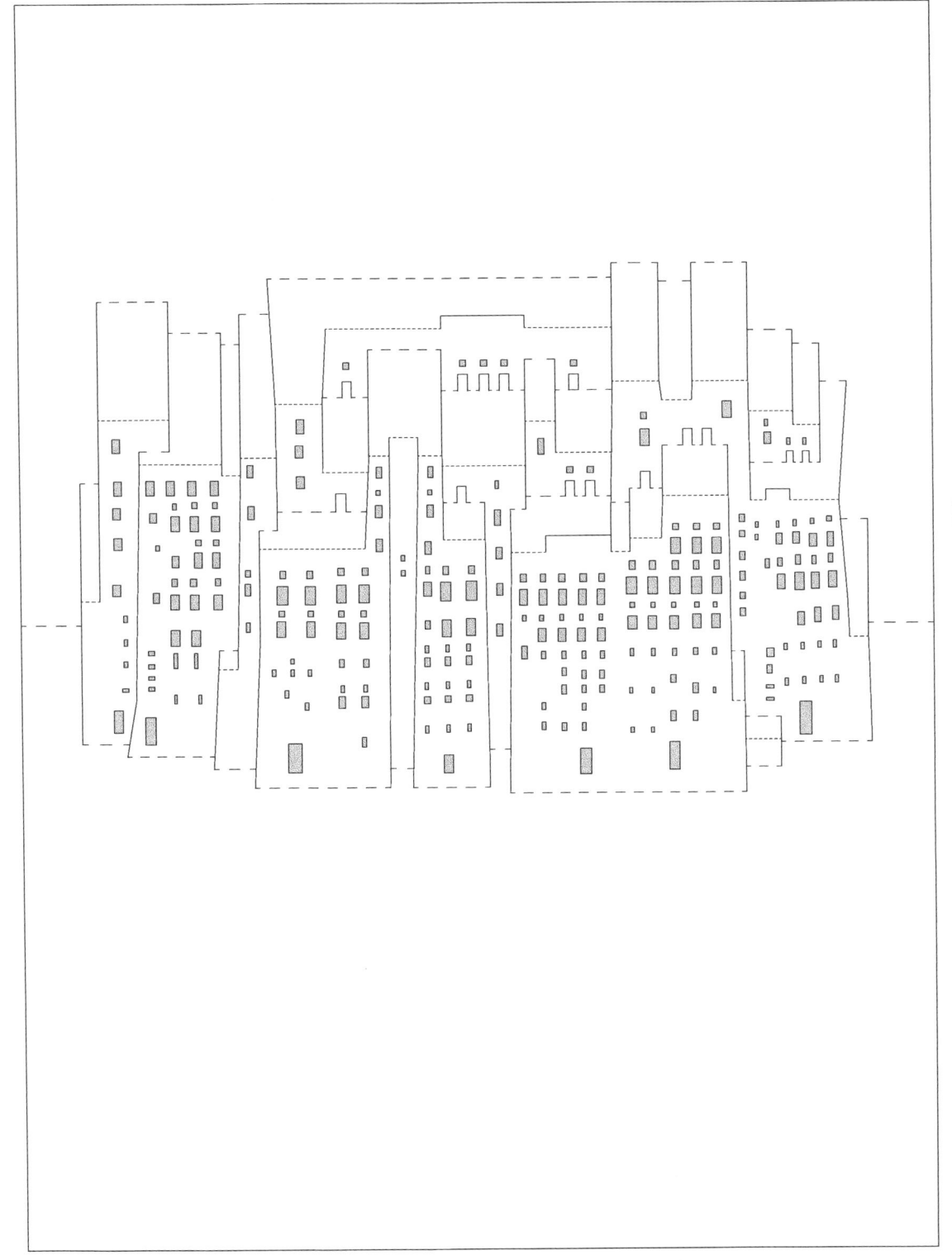

Asia

------ 山折り線 Ridge fold line　　--- 谷折り線 Valley fold line　　—— 切り線 Cutting line　　▨ 切り落し Cutout

23 タージ・マハル（インド）
Taj Mahal (India)

愛妻を偲ぶ皇帝によって建立された白い大理石ずくめの廟。涼しげな川に面してアベックの溜まり場となっている。白い紙に白い建築をつくる、究極の折り紙建築の愉しみを導いてくれるモチーフの一つです。

An emperor built this white marble mausoleum for his favorite wife. Today it attracts young lovers, who gather in the cool air of the adjacent river. The Taj Mahal affords the ultimate pleasure in origami building making—to construct a white building from white paper.

······ 山折り線 Ridge fold line　　--- 谷折り線 Valley fold line　　—— 切り線 Cutting line

24 アンコール・ワット（カンボジア）
Angkor Wat (Cambodia)

最も大きなアンコール遺跡。左右対称な外観は、遠目からもその巨大さと壮麗さが素晴らしく、一方、柱や壁面の浮彫り模様は大変繊細である。遠めで見てよし、近場で観察してよし。夕日さす連子窓の光と影は、日本の寺院建築を連想させる。

The beauty of Angkor Wat, the largest Angkor ruins, overwhelms from afar, with its symmetry, colossal size, and splendor, and from near, with its sensitive relief carvings in stone pillars and walls. Sunlight and shadow, cast at evening through lattice windows, suggest Japanese temple architecture.

------ 山折り線 Ridge fold line　--- 谷折り線 Valley fold line　—— 切り線 Cutting line　▯ 切り落し Cutout

25 ボロブドゥル寺院（インドネシア）
Borobudur (Indonesia)

1814年に発見された東洋のピラミッド、世界最大の仏教寺院。基壇の上に方形5層、円形3層からなり、東西南北の外側の階段から頂上まで登れるようになっている。

This Eastern "pyramid," discovered in 1814, is the largest Buddhist monument on earth. Above a high base are five square terraces and three concentric circular terraces. A staircase bisects each face, enabling one to climb to the top.

······ 山折り線 Ridge fold line   --- 谷折り線 Valley fold line   ── 切り線 Cutting line

26　万里の長城（中国）
The Great Wall (China)

紀元前6世紀に着工。秦の始皇帝によって築かれた要塞だが、この場に居ると龍に跨って空を翔るような気分。総全長は6,700km、まさにグレート・ウォール。

Work first began on the Great Wall in the 6th century BC. Although constructed as a stronghold by the First (Qin) Emperor, one feels as if astride a dragon, flying the sky, when here. At 6,700km in length, it is truly a "great wall."

------ 山折り線 Ridge fold line　--- 谷折り線 Valley fold line　—— 切り線 Cutting line

27 ポタラ宮 (中国)
Potala Palace (China)

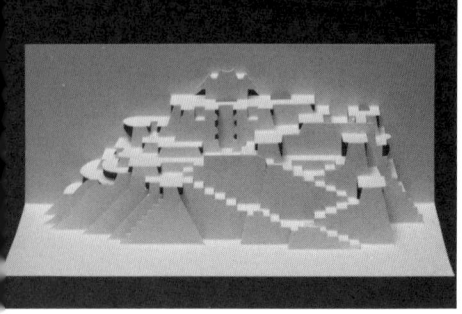

「垂直のベルサイユ」と称される、標高 3,600 m の山の頂上まで斜面に沿って建てられた高層建築。お参りは、時計回りに通路を巡り、中に入って五体投地、仏具「マニコル」を回せばよい。行く人は、高山病に気を付けましょう。

This "vertical Versailles" is a high-rise building constructed along the slope of a mountain summit 3,600m high. Devotees walk clockwise around its exterior passageways, throw themselves full-length on the ground upon entering, then rotate a Buddhist implement called a manikhor. Visitors should heed altitude sickness.

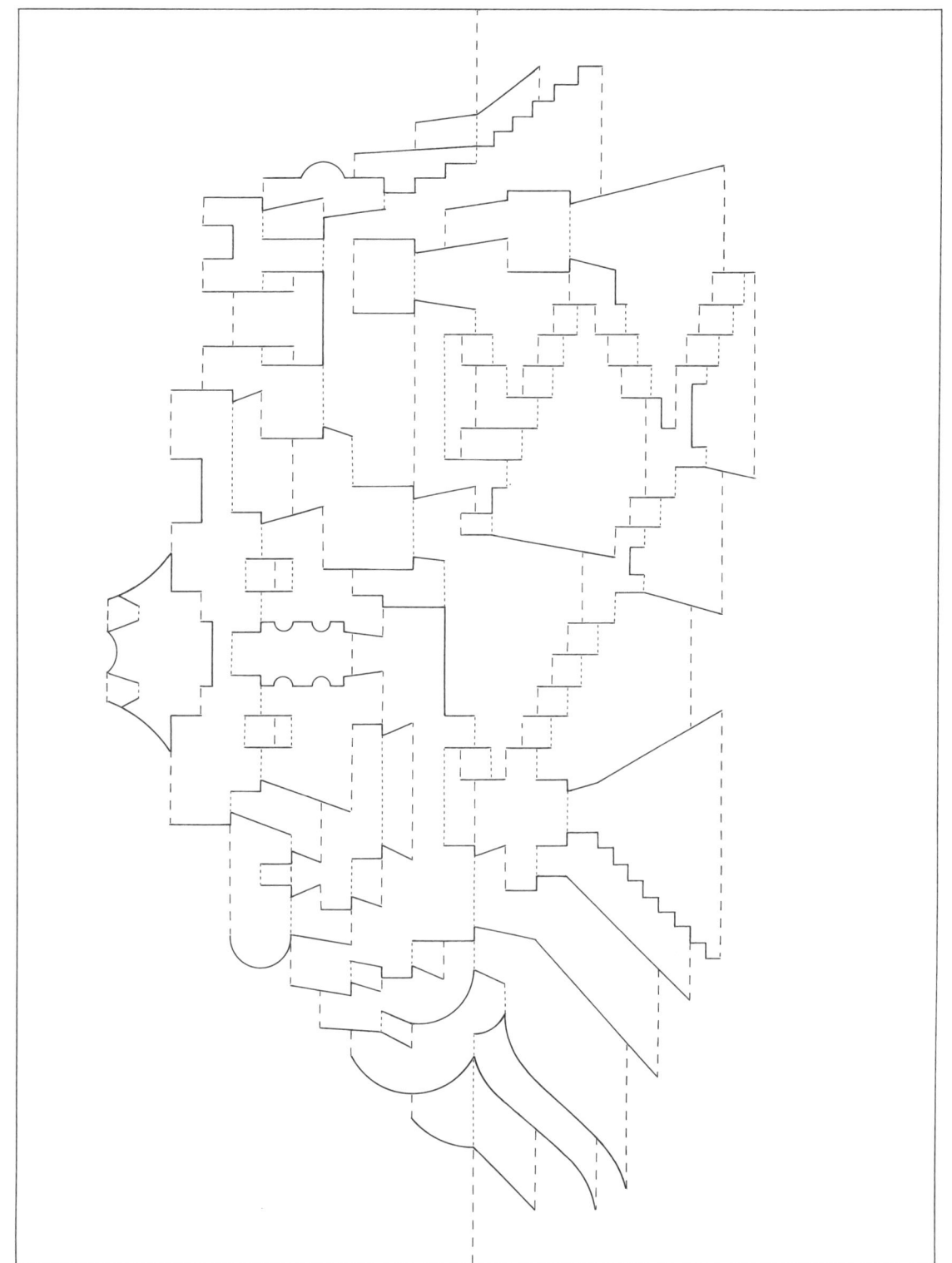

Asia

------ 山折り線 Ridge fold line   --- 谷折り線 Valley fold line   —— 切り線 Cutting line

28 昌徳宮 (韓国)
Changdeok Palace (Republic of Korea)

昌徳宮は、朝鮮王朝第3代王、太宗の時代の離宮として建てられた宮殿で、宗廟のすぐ北にある。正宮の景福宮が再建されるまでの270年間、正宮として使用され、仁政殿(正殿)では、国の重要行事が執り行われた。

Constructed as a detached palace in the time of Tae'jong, the 3rd Choson Dynasty monarch, Changdeok Palace served as the main palace for 270 years until Gyeongbok Palace was reconstructed. Important state ceremonies were held here at Injeongjeon Hall. Located directly north of Chongmyo Shrine.

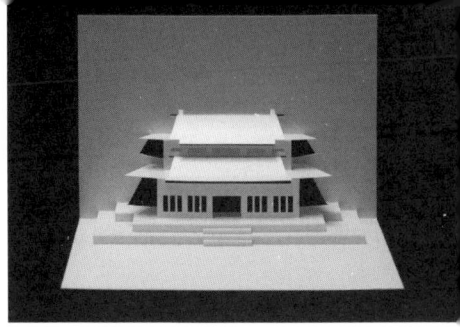

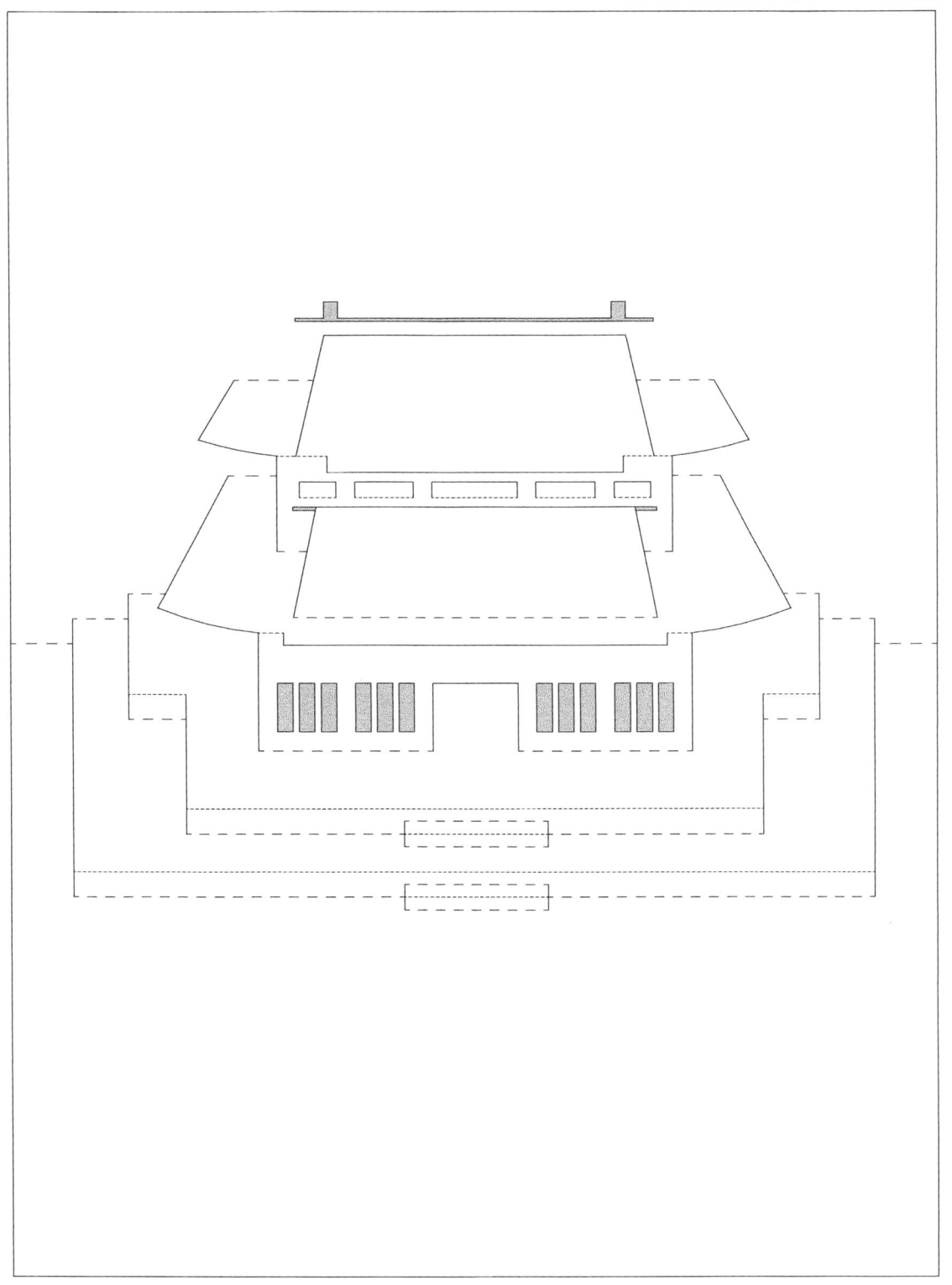

------ 山折り線 Ridge fold line   --- 谷折り線 Valley fold line   —— 切り線 Cutting line   ▓ 切り落し Cutout

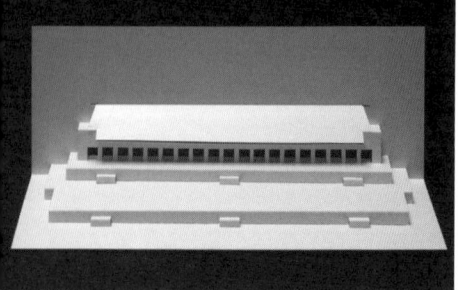

29 宗廟 (韓国)

Chongmyo Shrine (Republic of Korea)

ソウル市の中心にある宗廟は、朝鮮王朝歴代の王と王妃の霊廟。正殿は間口19間（約35 m）の長大な建築と、花崗岩敷の広い基壇からなる簡素な構成だが、朱塗りの列柱が緊張感のある雰囲気を生んでいる。

Chongmyo Shrine was built in central Seoul as a mausoleum for kings and queens of the Chosun Dynasty. The main shrine, a monumental structure of some 35m breadth on a granite foundation, has a simple composition yet its vermilion pillars produce a tense atmosphere.

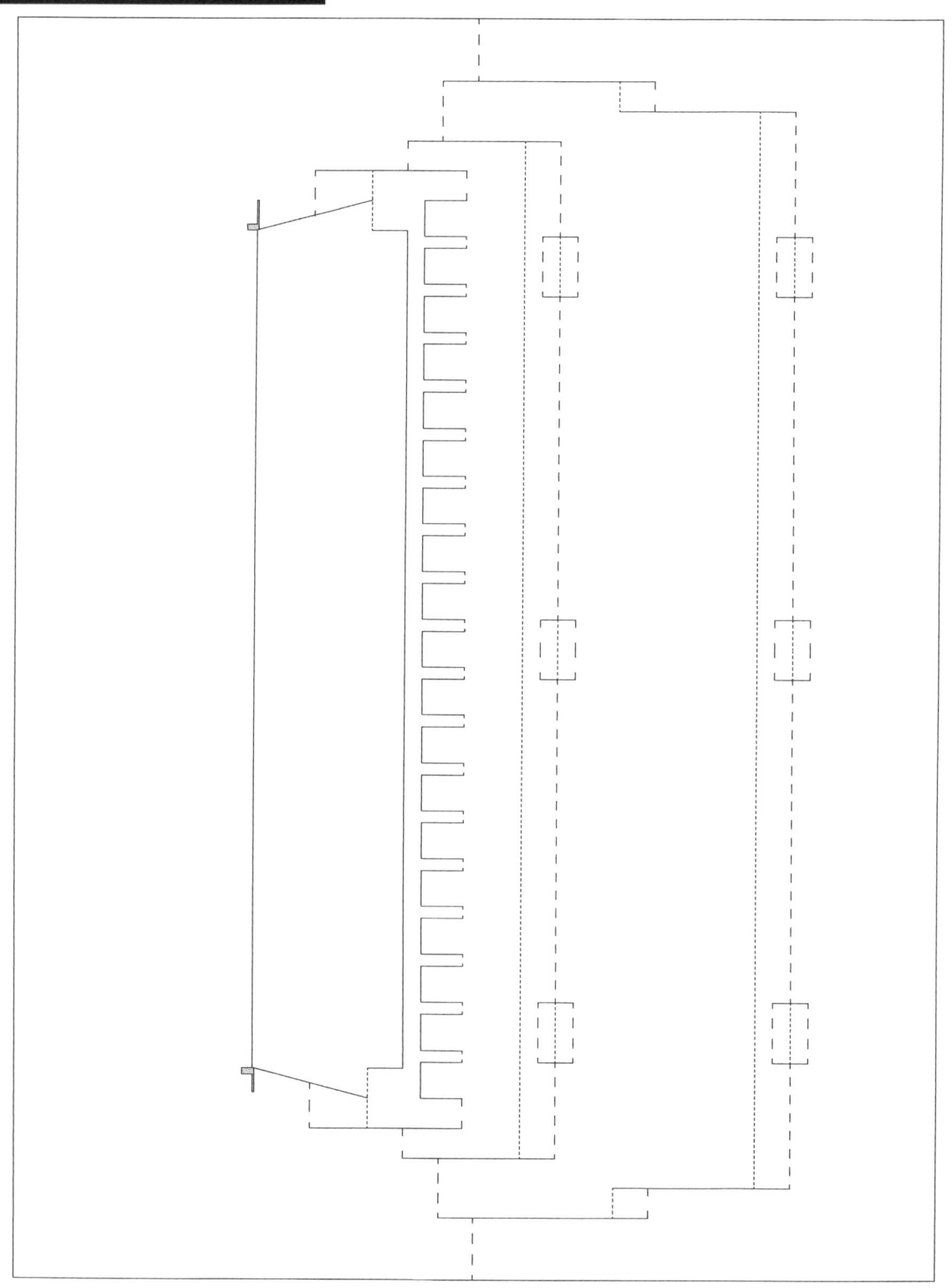

------ 山折り線 Ridge fold line　　--- 谷折り線 Valley fold line　　—— 切り線 Cutting line　　▨ 切り落し Cutout

30 姫路城（日本）
Himeji Castle (Japan)

別名「白鷺 城」とも呼ばれるお城の優美さの裏には、戦うための様々な優れた仕掛・機能があったと聞く。白漆喰も、銃弾に強く、耐火性にも優れているという防衛上の理由から採用された。

Beautiful Himeji Castle may be known as White Heron Castle, but it features many sophisticated contrivances for conducting war. Even its white plaster was employed for its resistance to bullets and fire.

------ 山折り線 Ridge fold line　　--- 谷折り線 Valley fold line　　—— 切り線 Cutting line　　▢ 切り落し Cutout

31 清水寺（日本）
Kiyomizu Temple (Japan)

現在の本堂は 1633 年に徳川家光によって再建された。内陣部分こそ地面に接するが、外陣と舞台は巨大な柱と貫だけで支えられて断崖上に建っている。谷越しに眺めると、大屋根を頂く「清水の舞台」が木々の合間に浮遊する。

Tokugawa Iemitsu built the present main hall in 1633. The inner temple sits on the ground, while the outer temple and stage stand above a precipice on massive posts and braces. From across the gorge, the Temple's great roof and stage seem to float among trees.

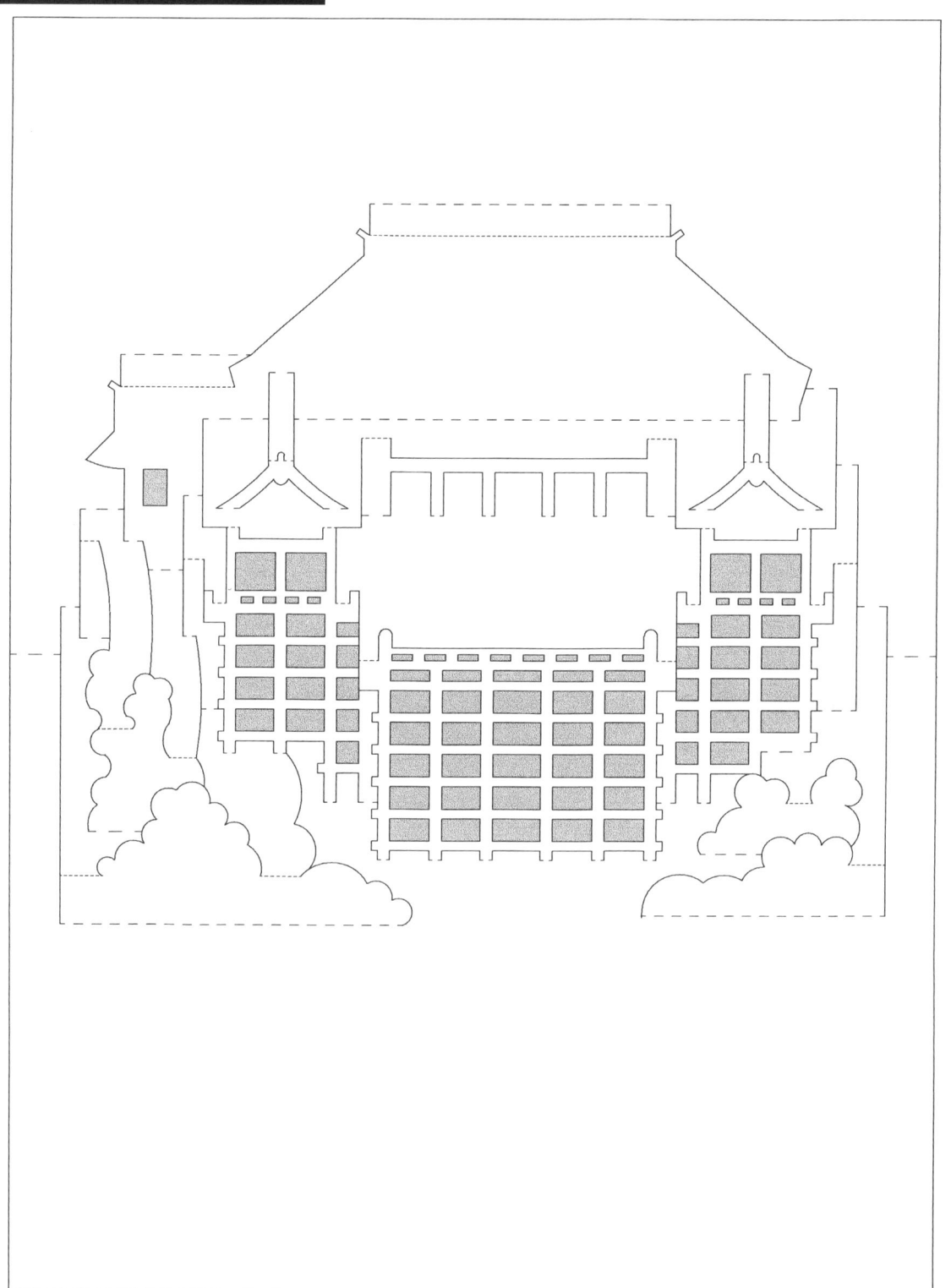

----- 山折り線 Ridge fold line --- 谷折り線 Valley fold line —— 切り線 Cutting line ▩ 切り落し Cutout

32　銀閣寺 （日本）
Ginkakuji (Japan)

足利8代将軍義政が京都東山につくった山荘のうち、慈照寺観音殿銀閣と称したもの。冬の雪を被った銀閣の姿を見たくて、足元の悪いなか、苦労して歩いたものである。

The Silver Pavilion, built by the 8th Ashikaga shogun, Yoshimasa, as part of his Higashiyama villa in Kyoto, is formally called Jisho-ji Kannon Chapel Ginkaku. Wanting to see it capped with winter snow, I walked into the compound, struggling to keep my footing.

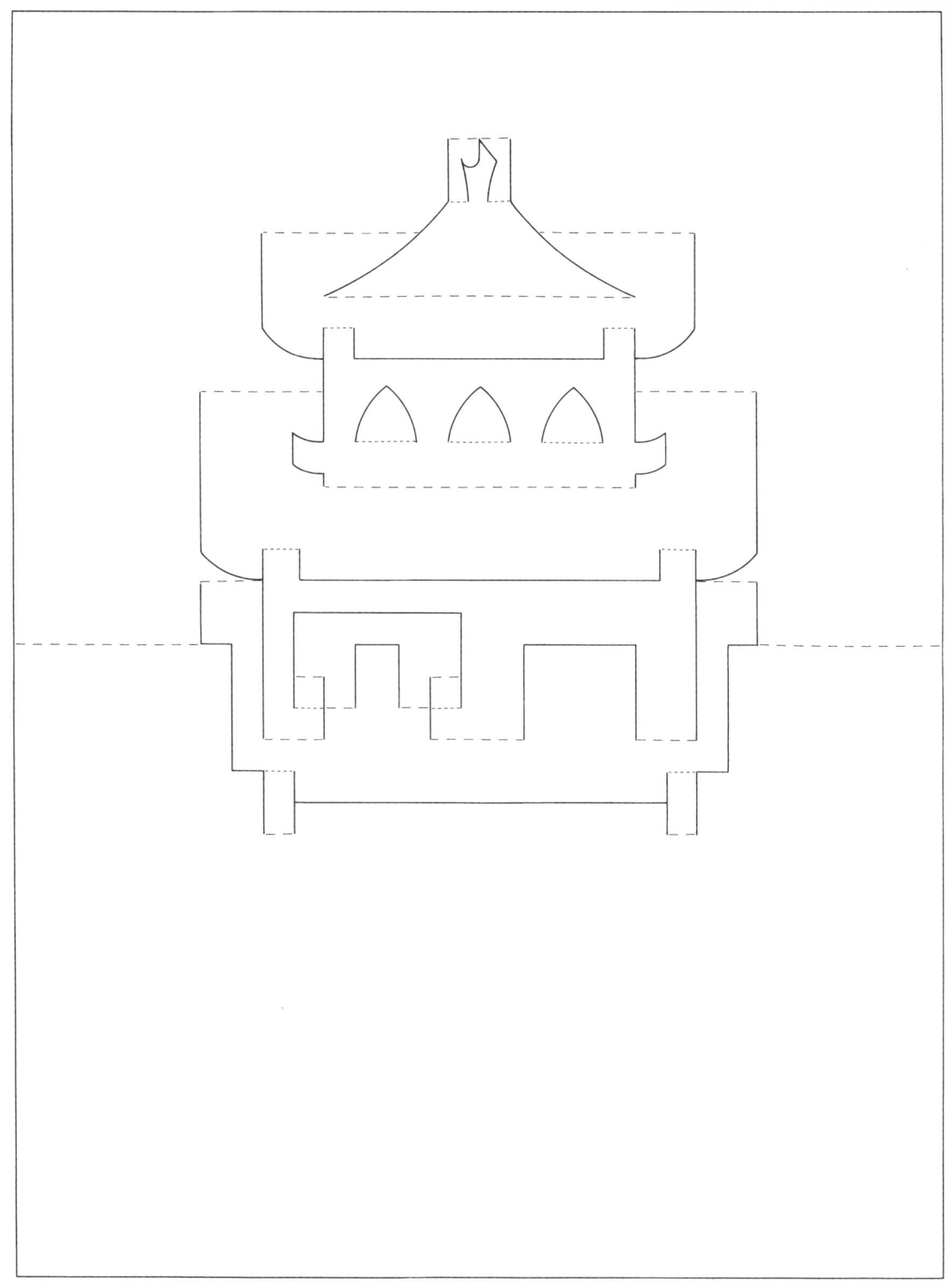

------ 山折り線 Ridge fold line　　--- 谷折り線 Valley fold line　　—— 切り線 Cutting line

49

33 平等院鳳凰堂 (日本)
Phoenix Hall of Byodo-in (Japan)

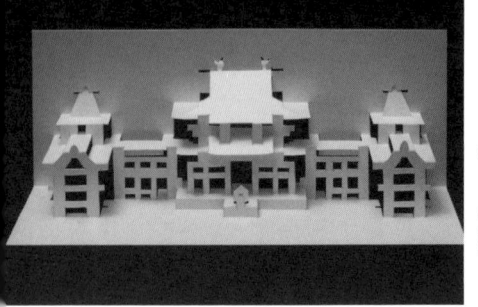

極楽浄土図をもとに当時の日本建築の粋を集めて建てられたお堂。細かい彫刻にも繧繝彩色が施され、壮麗な姿を池に映し続ける。

Phoenix Hall was built as a representation of Amida Buddha's Western Paradise, using the finest Japanese architectural techniques of its time. Colors are painted in graded shading on even small sculptures in the Phoenix Hall, and its lovely form stands reflected in a pond.

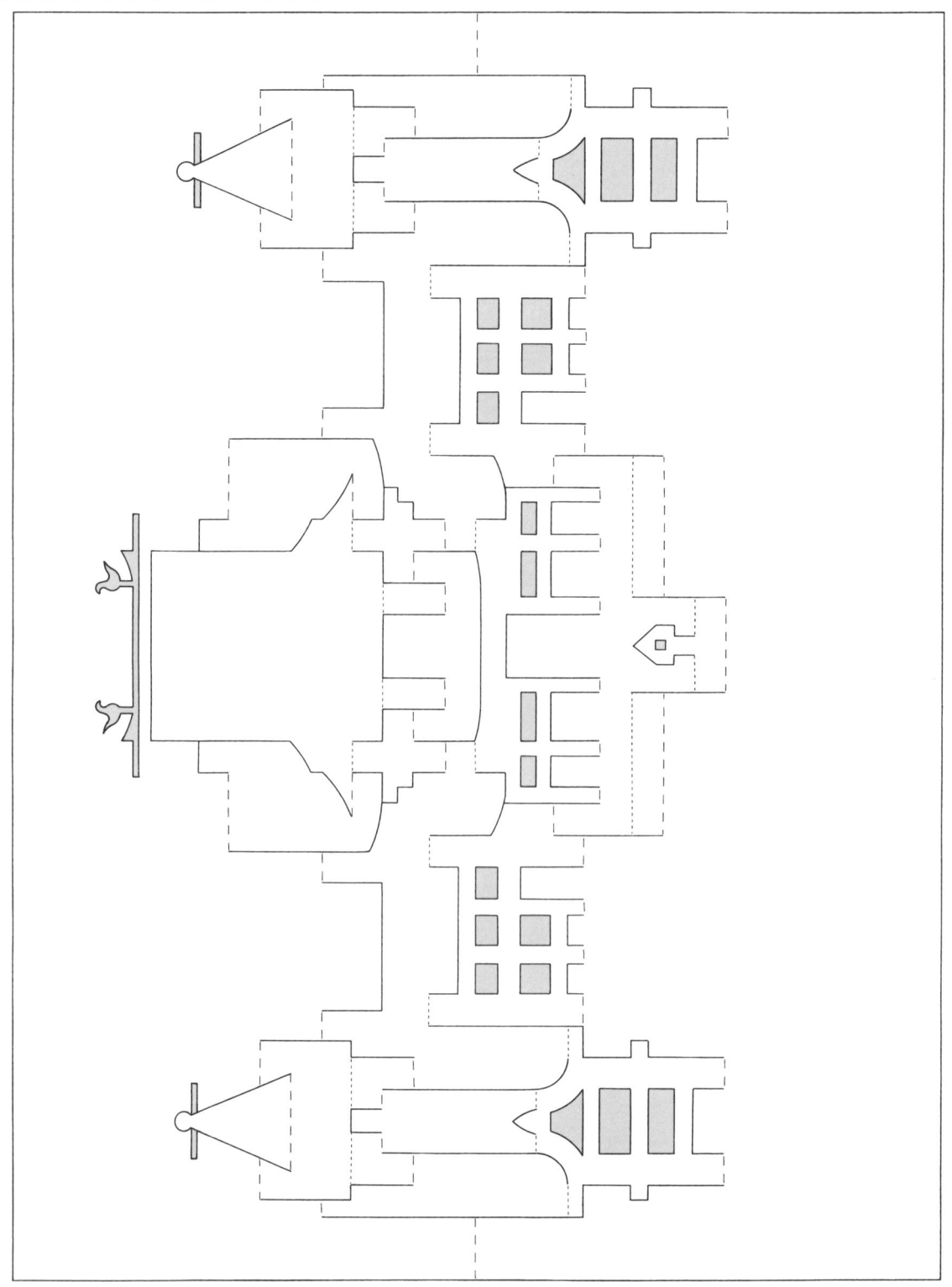

Asia

　･････ 山折り線 Ridge fold line　　--- 谷折り線 Valley fold line　　── 切り線 Cutting line　　▨ 切り落し Cutout

34 東寺五重塔（日本）
Toji Five-storied Pagoda (Japan)

京都の世界遺産で最も古い東寺は、796年に国の鎮護の寺として、都の入口の東西に建立されたが、西寺は焼失し東寺のみが残された。高さ57mの五重塔のシルエットは、平安の時代を偲ばせてくれる。

Toji, the oldest Kyoto World Heritage site, was built in 796 as a temple for "preserving and pacifying the country." Toji and Saiji once stood east and west of the city entrance, but Saiji burnt down, and only Toji remains today. Its 57m pagoda serenely recalls ancient Heian times.

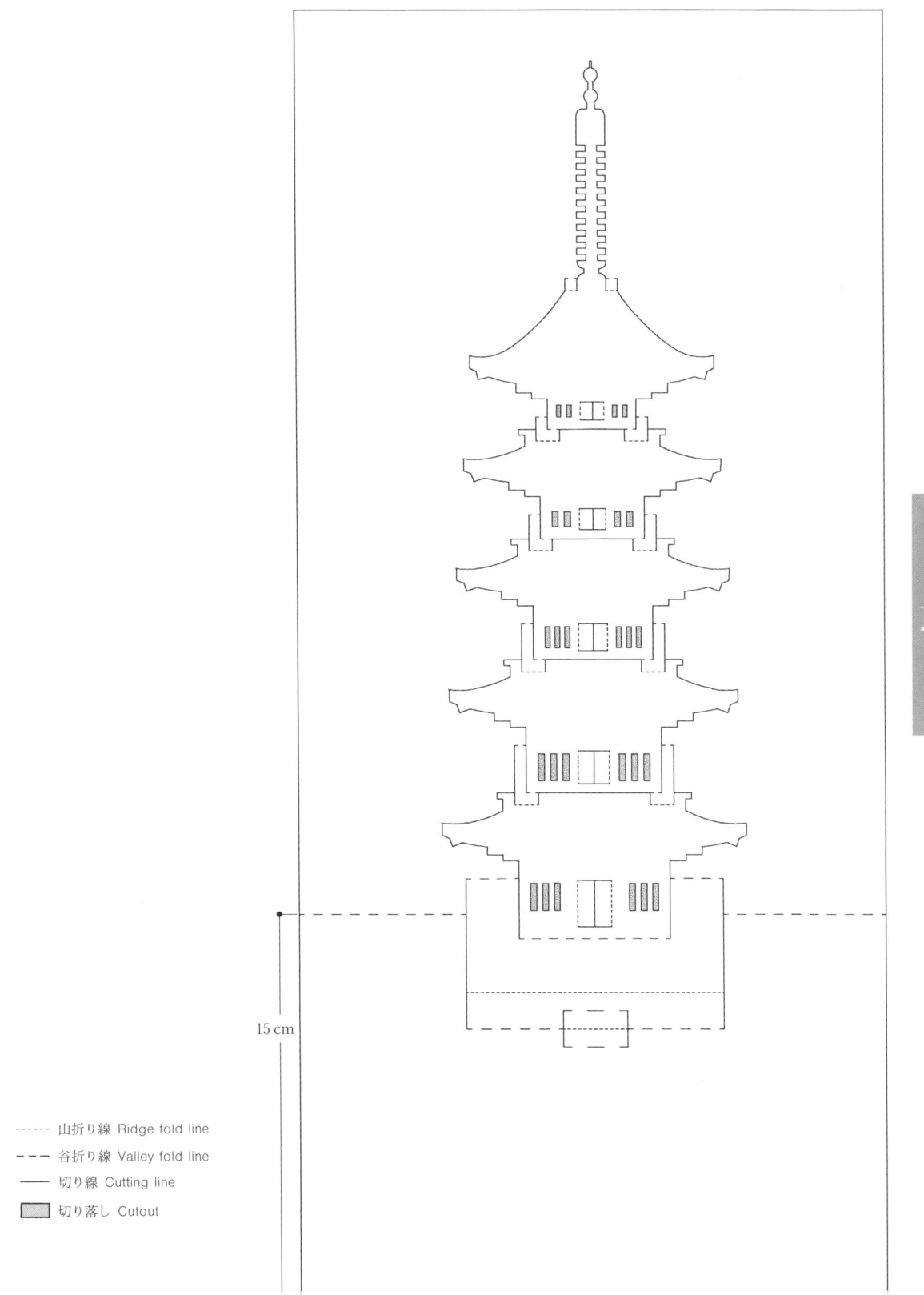

15 cm

- - - - - - 山折り線 Ridge fold line
- - - 谷折り線 Valley fold line
———— 切り線 Cutting line
▓▓ 切り落し Cutout

Asia

35 東大寺南大門（日本）
Todaiji Great South Gate (Japan)

現存する数少ない鎌倉時代の大仏様建築。高さ25.5ｍの丈と6段にわたる挿肘木で支える軒桁など、剛直な迫力がある。

One of the few surviving examples of "Indian style" (*tenjiku-yo*) architecture of Japan's Kamakura period. Its height of 25.5m and six tiers of bracket sets produce a mood of strength and integrity.

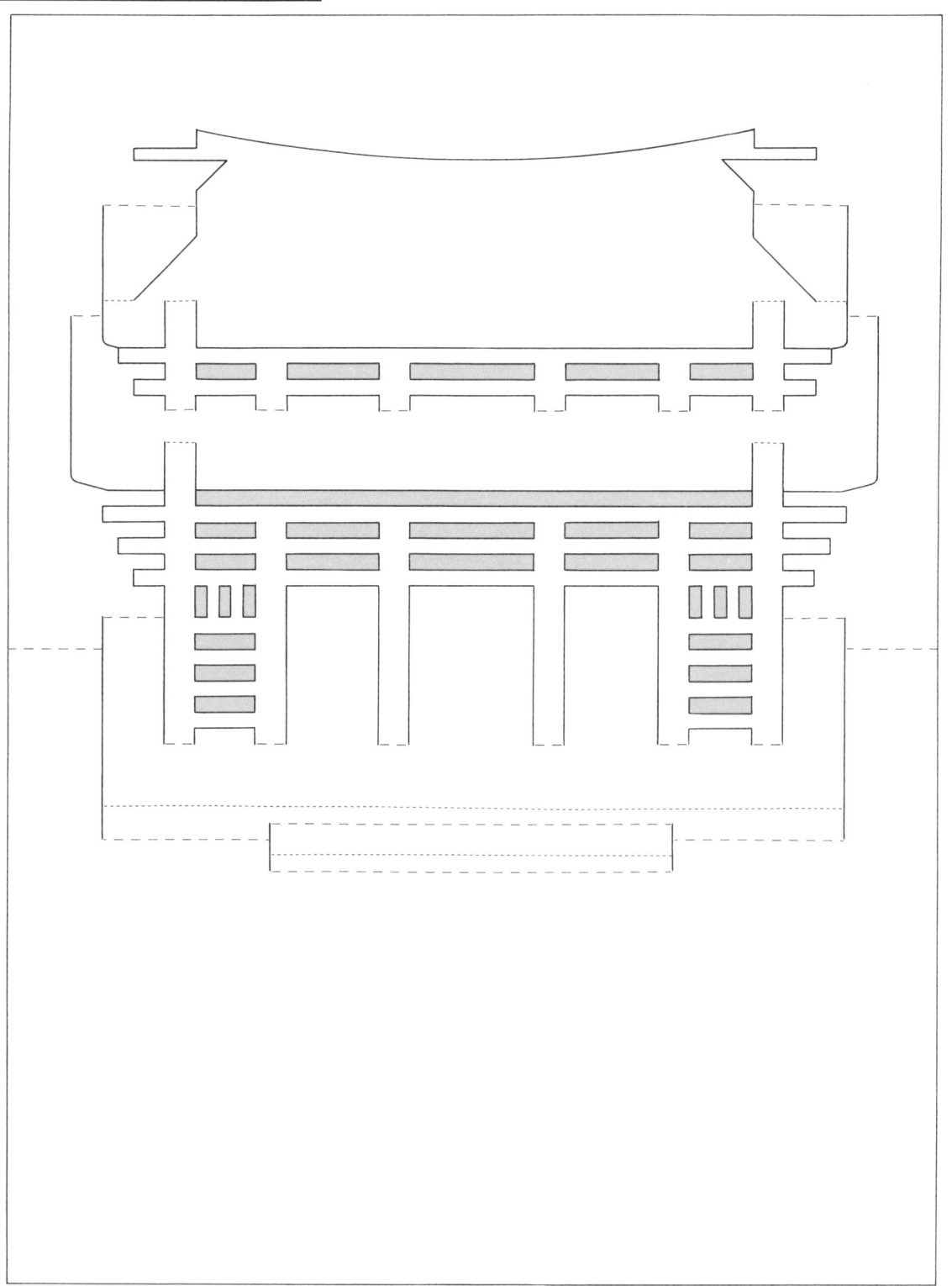

Asia

······ 山折り線 Ridge fold line   --- 谷折り線 Valley fold line   ── 切り線 Cutting line   ▥ 切り落し Cutout

36 合掌造り（日本）
Historic Villages of Shirakawa-go and Gokayama (Japan)

岐阜県の白川郷や富山県の五箇山に特有の民家は、60°もの逆Ｖ字の茅葺屋根と、2層から4層にもなる巨大な小屋裏空間、左右また四方の窓が特徴。両手を合わせた形に見えるので合掌造りと呼ぶ。

These characteristic farmhouses of Gifu and Toyama have steep thatched roofs, forming a 60° inverted V, and huge two- to four-level attics with windows on all or two sides. They are built in the Gassho (prayer) style, so called because their roofs suggest hands in prayer.

------ 山折り線 Ridge fold line　--- 谷折り線 Valley fold line　—— 切り線 Cutting line

37 首里城（日本）

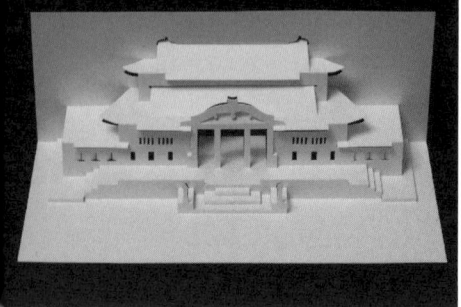

Shuri Castle (Japan)

琉球王朝のグスク（城塞）として登録された首里城跡は、焼失後に残った遺構や城塞のみだが、正殿・北殿・南殿と、鮮やかに復元された宮殿建築に、中国や日本の影響を受けながら、琉球独自の文化を育んできた歴史がうかがえる。

Only the foundation and portions of wall remain of Shuri Castle, which was destroyed by fire. Its colorful reconstructed State Hall and North and South Halls evoke the unique culture of the Ryukyus, which blended influences from China and Japan. Registered as a Gusuku (castle) site of the Kingdom of Ryukyu.

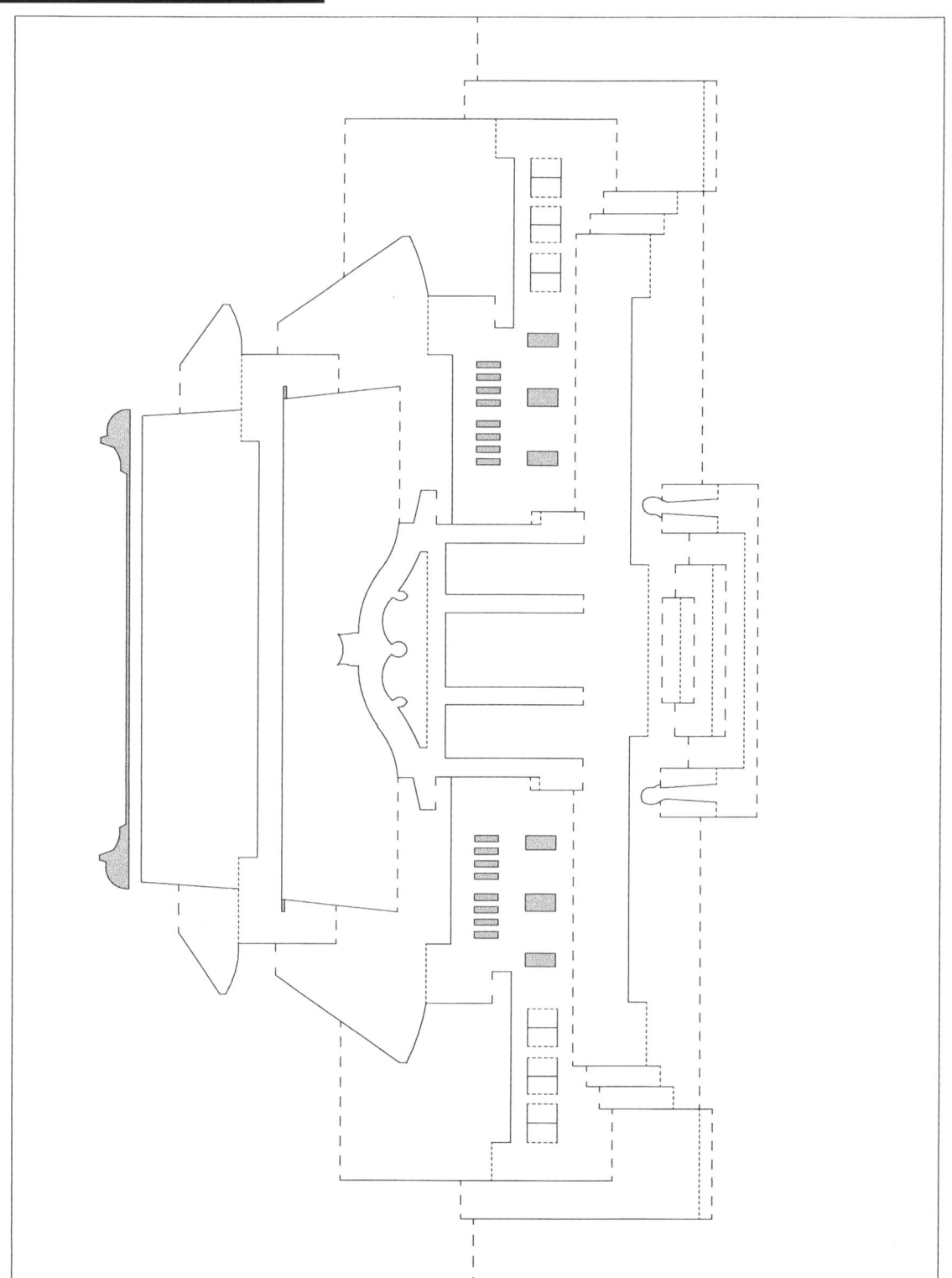

------ 山折り線 Ridge fold line　--- 谷折り線 Valley fold line　——— 切り線 Cutting line　▨ 切り落し Cutout

38 自由の女神像（アメリカ合衆国）
Statue of Liberty (United States)

自由の女神像は、アメリカ合衆国の独立100年を記念して、1886年にフランスから贈られたもの。左手に独立宣言書、右手に希望の松明を掲げ、宝冠の突起が7つの海と大陸に広がる様は、自由と希望と民主主義の象徴。

France presented this statue to the United States in 1886 for its centennial. With the declaration of independence in her left hand, the torch of hope in her right, and the spikes of her crown radiating to the seven oceans and continents, the statue symbolizes freedom, hope, and democracy.

15 cm

------ 山折り線 Ridge fold line
--- 谷折り線 Valley fold line
—— 切り線 Cutting line

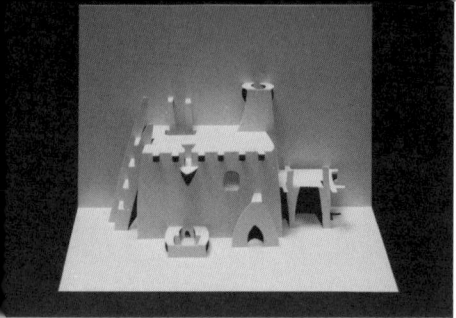

39 タオス・プエブロ （アメリカ合衆国）
Taos Pueblo (United States)

アメリカ先住民の家。土と日干し煉瓦でつくられている。煙突や梯子など、細かいところが楽しいつくりになっている。

These Native American houses are built using mud and sun-dried adobe bricks. Such details as the chimneys and ladders give pleasure to the eye.

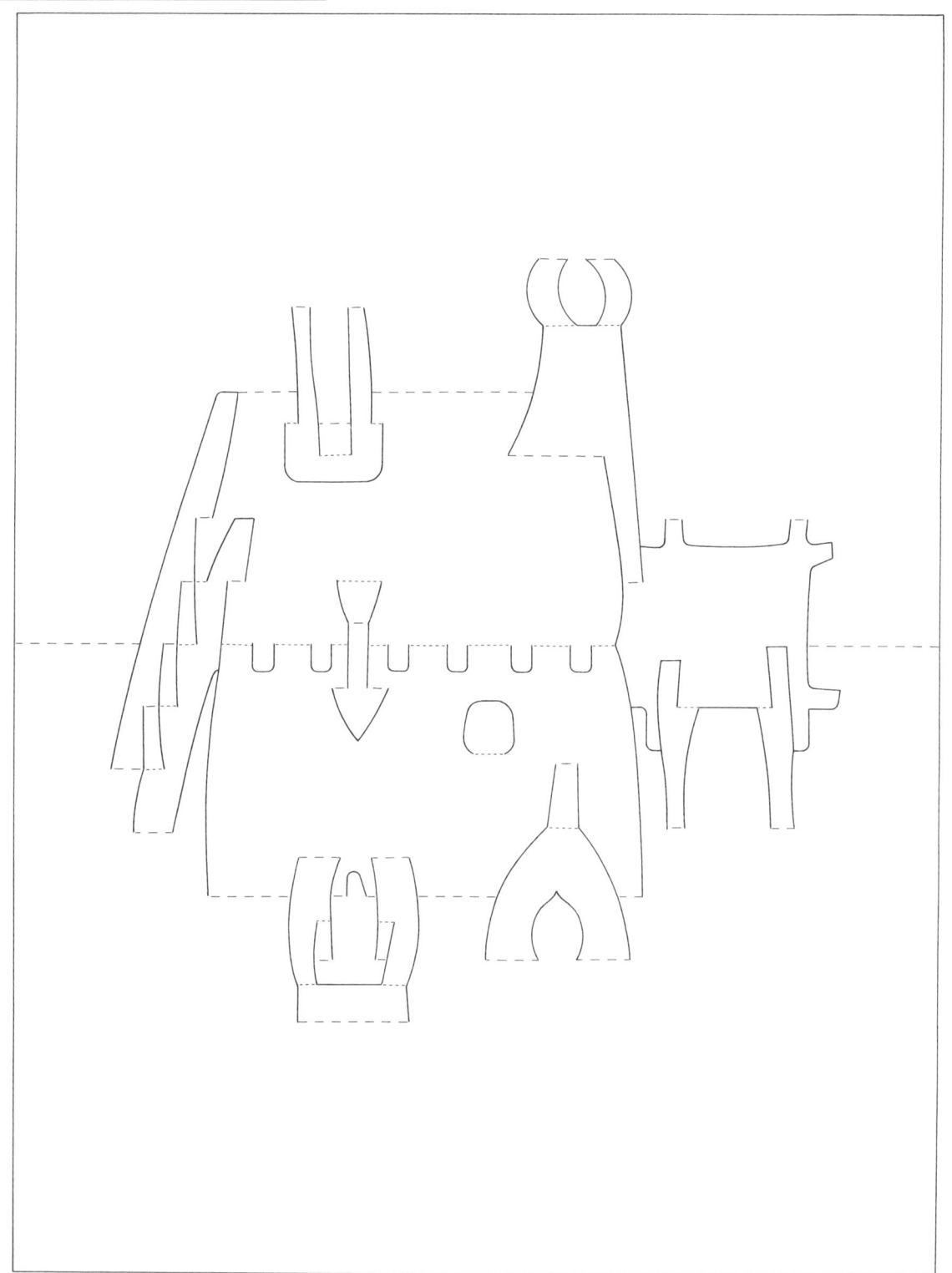

······ 山折り線 Ridge fold line　　− − − 谷折り線 Valley fold line　　——— 切り線 Cutting line

40　魔法使いのピラミッド（メキシコ）
Pyramid of the Magician (Mexico)

マヤのピラミッドはもともと神を祀る場所。魔法使いが一日で建てたといわれる伝説のピラミッドは、平面が楕円に近く丸みを帯びた珍しいもの。ククルカンのピラミッドとは対照的に、素朴なマヤ文明の姿を伝えてくれる。

Mayan pyramids were sacred places for worship. This pyramid which, according to legend, was built by a magician in one night, has an unusual rounded plan that is nearly oval. Unlike the pyramid of Kukulkan, it expresses the simple purity of Mayan civilization.

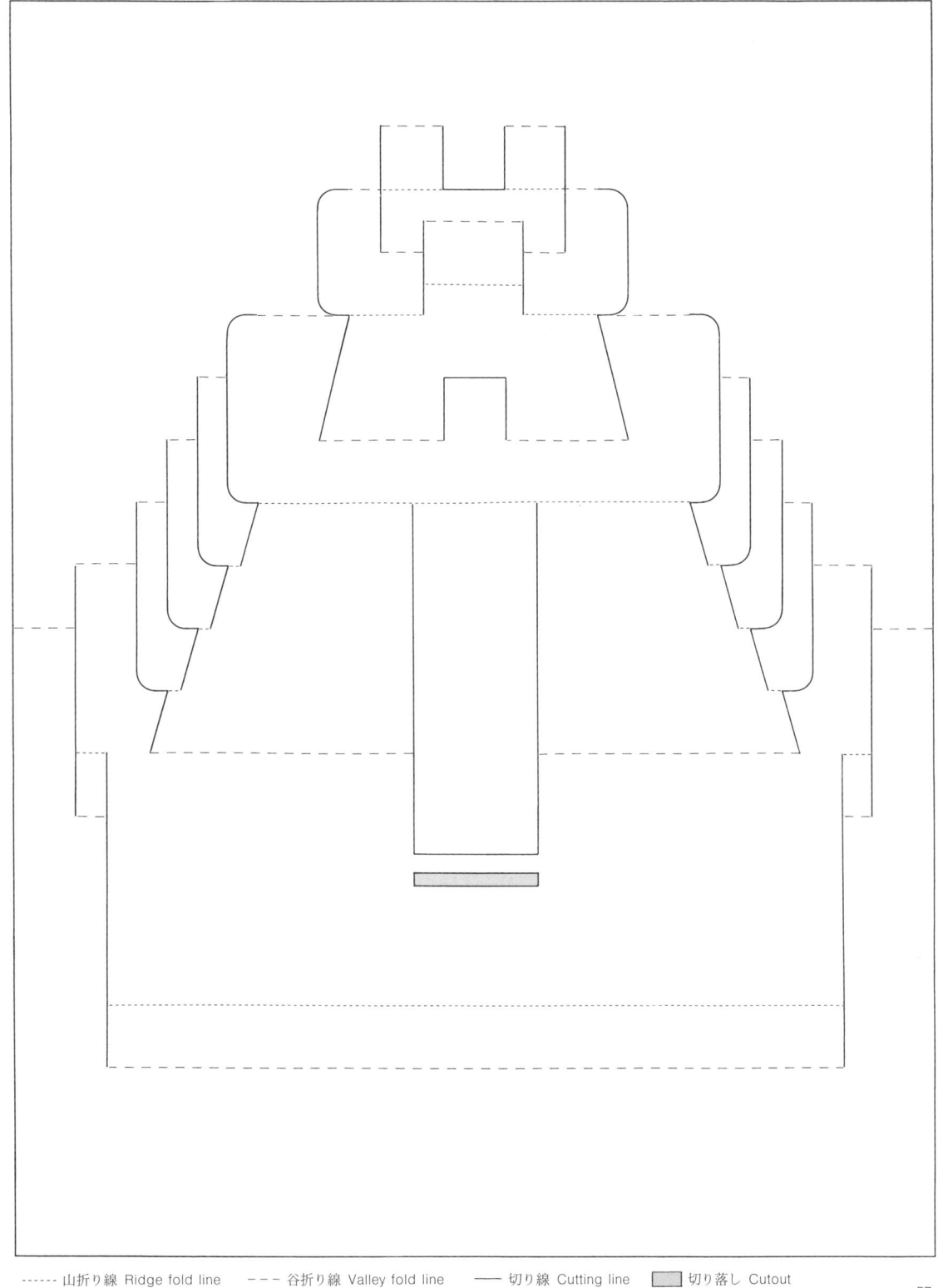

------ 山折り線 Ridge fold line　--- 谷折り線 Valley fold line　—— 切り線 Cutting line　▧ 切り落し Cutout

41 ハバナ大聖堂（キューバ）

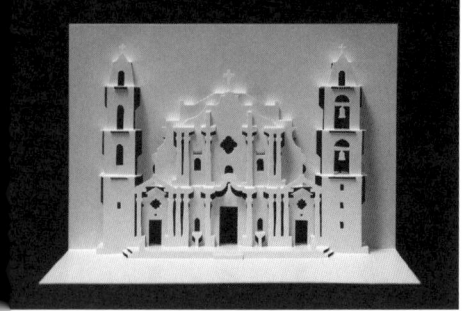

Havana Cathedral (Cuba)

ハバナ旧市街の中心にある大聖堂は、1767年頃の完成。キューバを代表するバロック建築である。ヨーロッパの世界進出が盛んだったこの時期、各地の植民都市には多くのバロック様式の建築が建てられた。

This cathedral in the heart of Old Havana was completed around 1767. Its baroque style is representative of Cuban architecture of the colonial period, when the European empires were at their apogee, and baroque buildings were built in colonial cities around the world.

------ 山折り線 Ridge fold line　--- 谷折り線 Valley fold line　—— 切り線 Cutting line　▭ 切り落し Cutout

42 サン・ニコラス・デ・バリ病院 (ドミニカ共和国)
San Nicolás de Bari Hospital (Dominican Republic)

コロンブス第1回航海で発見の新大陸で最初につくられた、ドミニカ共和国の首都サント・ドミンゴ。旧市街全体に新大陸時代の面影や遺跡が点在する。ここも新大陸最古の病院の遺跡というわけである。

Santo Domingo, the Dominican Republic's capital, was the first settlement founded in the Americas, after Columbus's first voyage. The entire old city quarter is dotted with sights and ruins suggestive of the days of conquest, among them these ruins of the new world's oldest hospital.

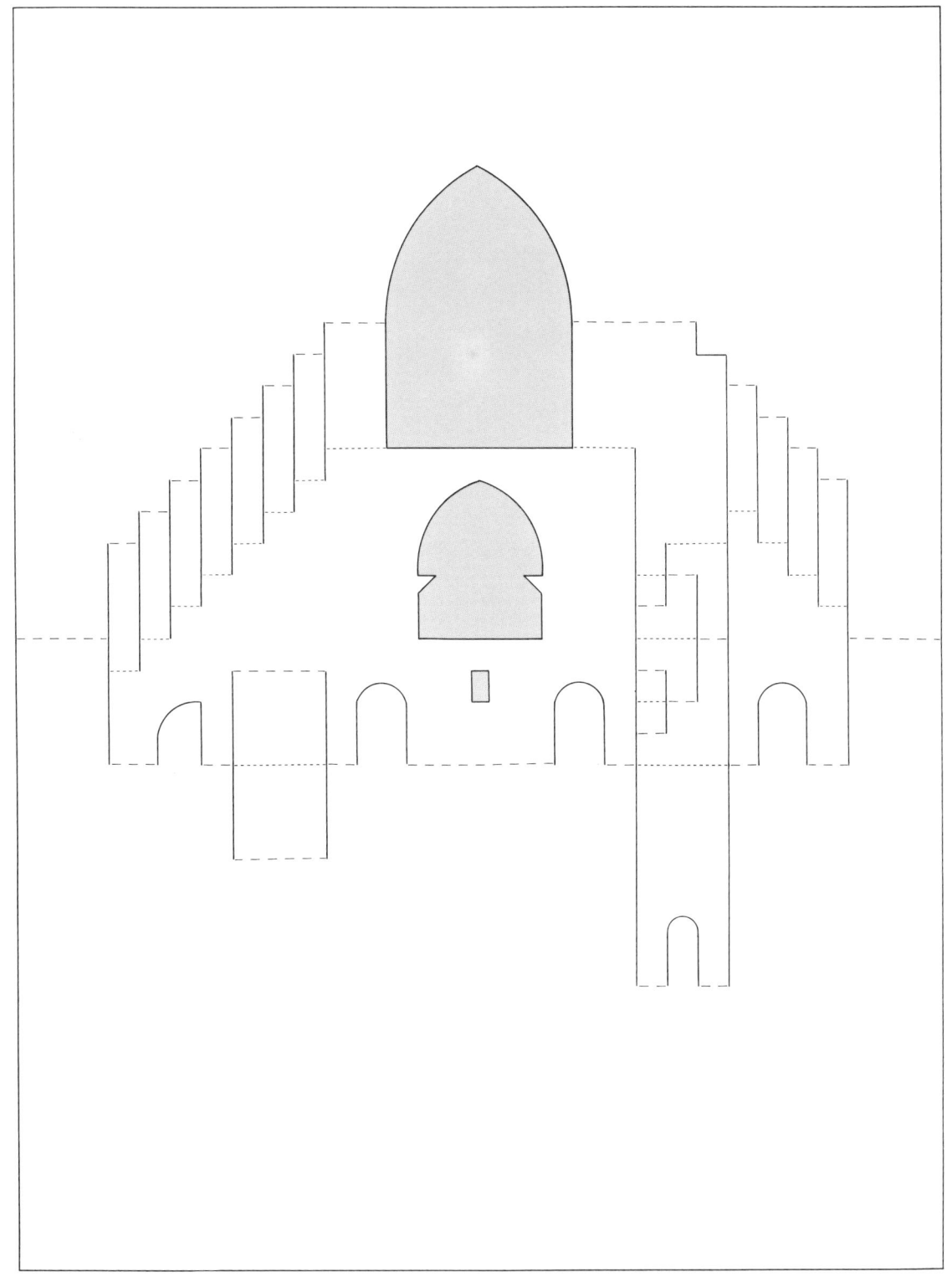

------ 山折り線 Ridge fold line　--- 谷折り線 Valley fold line　―― 切り線 Cutting line　▨ 切り落し Cutout

43 マチュピチュ（ペルー）
Machu Picchu (Peru)

「老いた峰」という意味の空中都市マチュピチュは、標高 2,280 m の山の頂にある。完璧に製材化された大きな石を組み上げた技術、高度な文明は、400 年も人目に触れずにいた。謎だらけである。

Machu Picchu, a city in the sky whose name means "old peak," sits on a mountain ridge 2,280m high. Its existence was unknown for 400 years. The sophisticated civilization that built it and the methods used to assemble large, exactly milled stones are still veiled in mystery.

・・・・・ 山折り線 Ridge fold line   --- 谷折り線 Valley fold line   —— 切り線 Cutting line

44 モアイ（チリ）
Moais (Chile)

「世界のへそ」に位置する南米チリのイースター島には、12〜15世紀につくられたとされる1,000体ものモアイ像がある。その3分の1は胴体部分だけのつくりかけだが、最大で高さ20 mになるものも。

On Easter Island, a Chilean island in the south Pacific known as the "navel of the world," there are 1,000 stone Moai statues created in the 12th to 15th centuries. A third of them are just torsos, but the largest stand up to 20m high.

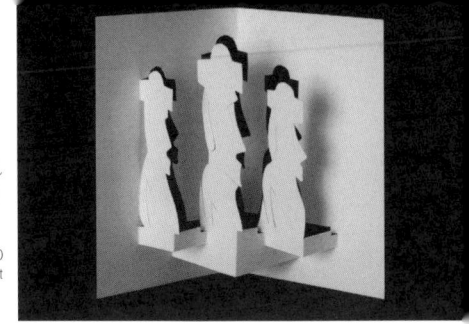

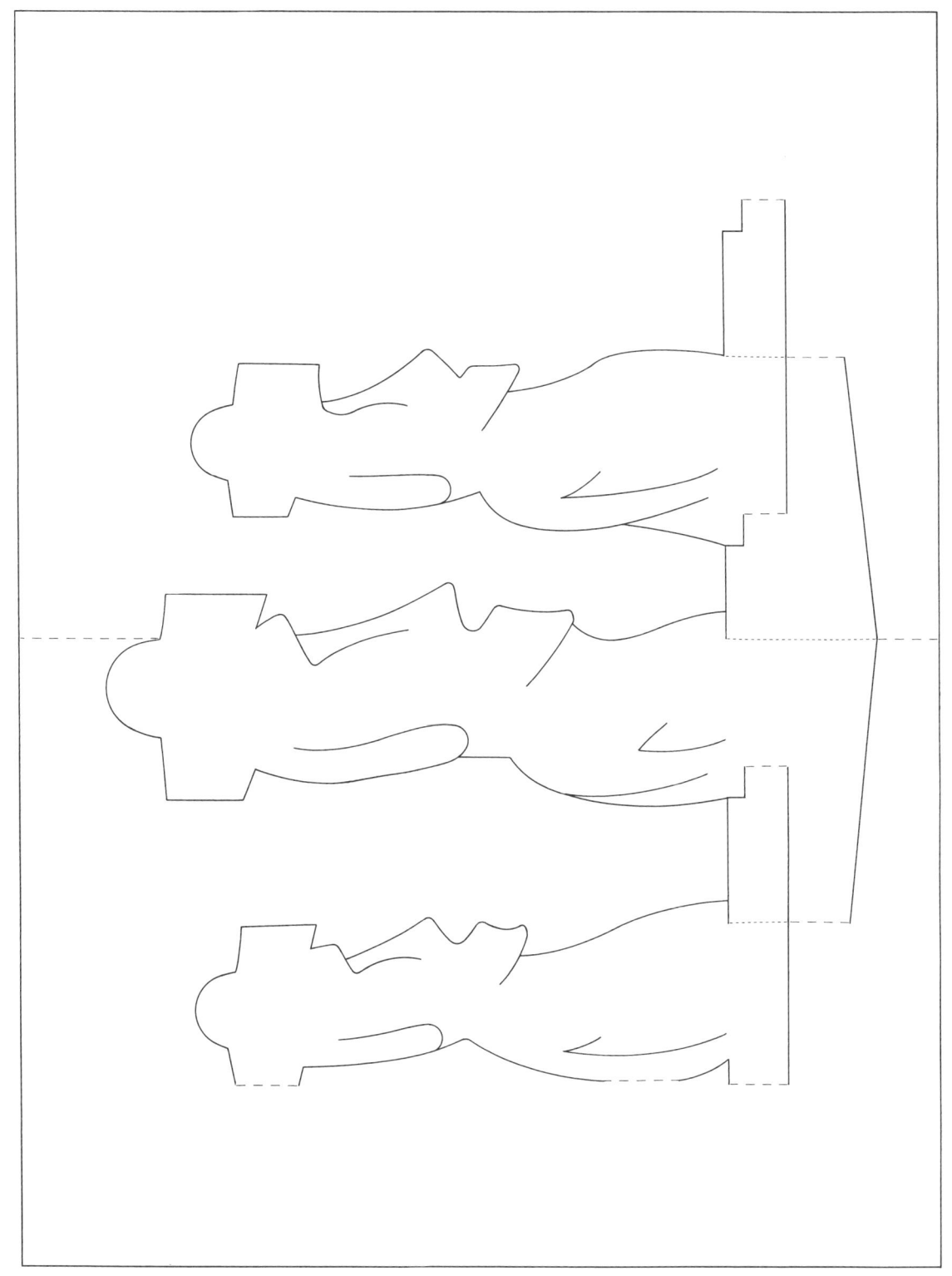

------ 山折り線 Ridge fold line　---- 谷折り線 Valley fold line　—— 切り線 Cutting line

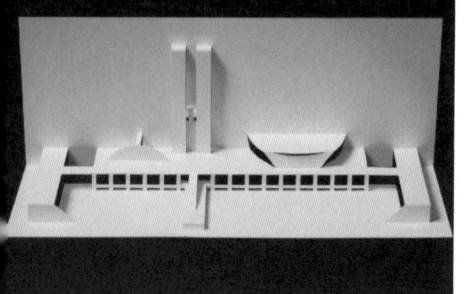

45　ブラジリアの国会議事堂（ブラジル）
Congress Building, Brasilia (Brazil)

ブラジリアは、セラードという何もない荒野に、わずか4年で築かれた新首都。ユニークな国会議事堂を形づくるドーム屋根は上院、ドームを逆さにした方が下院。上下両院で地球を現している。

In just four years Brazil built a new capital, Brasila, in the wild savanna of Cerrado. Its distinctive Congress Building consists of a Senate with a domed roof and a Chamber of Deputies under an inverted dome. Together, the two governmental houses express a complete sphere.

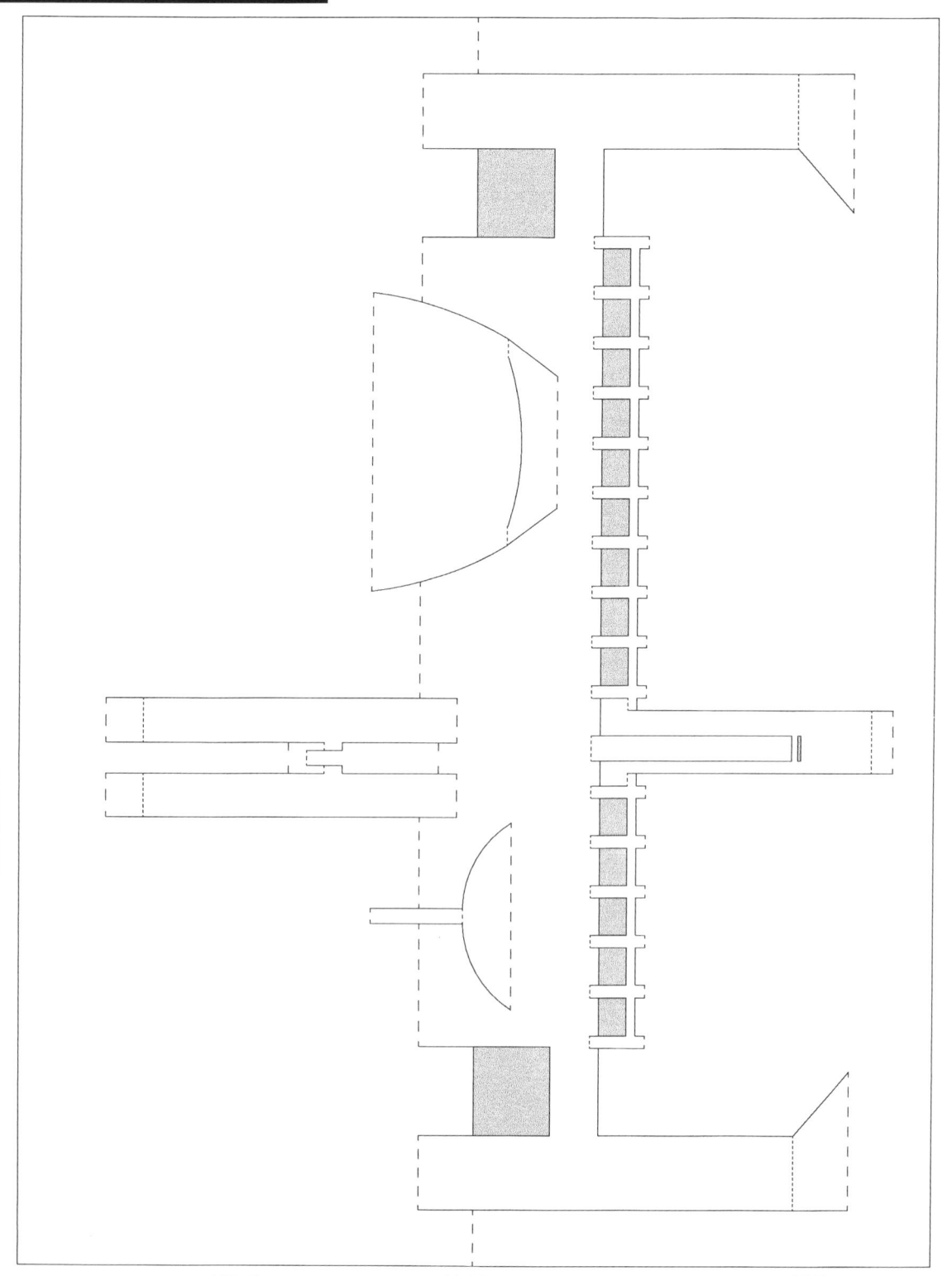

------ 山折り線 Ridge fold line　--- 谷折り線 Valley fold line　—— 切り線 Cutting line　▒ 切り落し Cutout

この本の世界遺産名・登録年

1 ピラミッド（エジプト）
遺産名　メンフィスとその墓地遺跡、ギザからダハシュールまでのピラミッド地帯
登録年　1979年

2 アブ・シンベル神殿（エジプト）
遺産名　アブ・シンベルからフィラエまでのヌビア遺跡群
登録年　1979年

3 グレート・ジンバブエ（ジンバブエ）
遺産名　大ジンバブエ国立記念物
登録年　1986年

4 ジェンネの大モスク（マリ）
遺産名　ジェンネの旧市街
登録年　1988年

5 アルベロベッロのトゥルッリ（イタリア）
遺産名　アルベロベッロのトゥルッリ
登録年　1996年

6 サンタ・マリア・デル・フィオーレ大聖堂（イタリア）
遺産名　フィレンツェ歴史地区
登録年　1982年

7 ヴィラ・ロトンダ（イタリア）
遺産名　ヴィチェンツァ市街とヴェネト地方のパラーディオ様式の邸宅群
登録年　1994/1996年

8 ベレンの塔（ポルトガル）
遺産名　リスボンのジェロニモス修道院とベレンの塔
登録年　1983年

9 エッフェル塔（フランス）
遺産名　パリのセーヌ河岸
登録年　1991年

10 ノートル・ダム大聖堂（フランス）
遺産名　パリのセーヌ河岸
登録年　1991年

11 ウェストミンスター修道院（イギリス）
遺産名　ウェストミンスター宮殿と修道院およびセント・マーガレット教会
登録年　1987年

12 アイアンブリッジ（イギリス）
遺産名　アイアンブリッジ峡谷
登録年　1986年

13 ベルリンの博物館島・旧博物館（ドイツ）
遺産名　ベルリンのムゼウムスインゼル
登録年　1999年

14 リラ修道院（ブルガリア）
遺産名　リラ修道院
登録年　1983年

15 ザカリアス広場の家並み（チェコ）
遺産名　テルチ歴史地区
登録年　1992年

16 パルテノン神殿（ギリシア）
遺産名　アテネのアクロポリス
登録年　1987年

17 メテオラの修道院（ギリシア）
遺産名　メテオラ
登録年　1988年

18 キジ島の木造教会（ロシア）
遺産名　キジ島の木造教会
登録年　1990年

19 アヤ・ソフィア（トルコ）
遺産名　イスタンブール歴史地域
登録年　1985年

20 カッパドキアの洞窟聖堂（トルコ）
遺産名　ギョレメ国立公園とカッパドキアの岩窟群
登録年　1985年

21 ハトラ遺跡（イラク）
遺産名　ハトラ
登録年　1985年

22 シバームの旧城壁都市（イエメン）
遺産名　シバームの旧城壁都市
登録年　1982年

23 タージ・マハル（インド）
遺産名　タージ・マハル
登録年　1983年

24	アンコール・ワット（カンボジア） 遺産名　アンコール 登録年　1992年	36	合掌造り（日本） 遺産名　白川郷・五箇山の合掌造り集落 登録年　1995年
25	ボロブドゥル寺院（インドネシア） 遺産名　ボロブドゥル寺院遺跡群 登録年　1991年	37	首里城（日本） 遺産名　琉球王国のグスクおよび関連遺産群 登録年　2000年
26	万里の長城（中国） 遺産名　万里の長城 登録年　1987年	38	自由の女神像（アメリカ合衆国） 遺産名　自由の女神像 登録年　1984年
27	ポタラ宮（中国） 遺産名　ラサのポタラ宮歴史地区群 登録年　1994/2000/2001年	39	タオス・プエブロ（アメリカ） 遺産名　タオスの先住民集落 登録年　1992年
28	昌徳宮（韓国） 遺産名　昌徳宮 登録年　1997年	40	魔法使いのピラミッド（メキシコ） 遺産名　古代都市ウシュマル 登録年　1996年
29	宗廟（韓国） 遺産名　宗廟 登録年　1995年	41	ハバナ大聖堂（キューバ） 遺産名　ハバナの旧市街と要塞 登録年　1982年
30	姫路城（日本） 遺産名　姫路城 登録年　1993年	42	サン・ニコラス・デ・バリ病院（ドミニカ共和国） 遺産名　サント・ドミンゴの植民都市 登録年　1990年
31	清水寺（日本） 遺産名　古都京都の文化財 登録年　1994年	43	マチュピチュ（ペルー） 遺産名　マチュピチュの歴史保護区 登録年　1983年
32	銀閣寺（日本） 遺産名　古都京都の文化財 登録年　1994年	44	モアイ（チリ） 遺産名　ラパ・ヌイ（イースター島）国立公園 登録年　1995年
33	平等院鳳凰堂（日本） 遺産名　古都京都の文化財 登録年　1994年	45	ブラジリアの国会議事堂（ブラジル） 遺産名　ブラジリア 登録年　1987年
34	東寺五重塔（日本） 遺産名　古都京都の文化財 登録年　1994年		
35	東大寺南大門（日本） 遺産名　古都奈良の文化財 登録年　1998年		

World Heritage Sites Appearing in This Book : Official Name and Year of Registration

1 Pyramids (Egypt)
Name: Memphis and its Necropolis—the Pyramid Fields from Giza to Dahshur
Year: 1979

2 Abu Simbel (Egypt)
Name: Nubian Monuments from Abu Simbel to Philae
Year: 1979

3 Great Zimbabwe (Zimbabwe)
Name: Great Zimbabwe National Monument
Year: 1986

4 Great Mosque of Djenné (Mali)
Name: Old Towns of Djenné
Year: 1988

5 Trulli of Alberobello (Italy)
Name: The Trulli of Alberobello
Year: 1996

6 Santa Maria del Fiore (Italy)
Name: Historic Centre of Florence
Year: 1982

7 Villa Rotonda (Italy)
Name: City of Vicenza and the Palladian Villas of the Veneto
Year: 1994, 1996

8 Belém Tower (Portugal)
Name: Monastery of the Hieronymites and Tower of Belém in Lisbon
Year: 1983

9 Eiffel Tower (France)
Name: Paris, Banks of the Seine
Year: 1991

10 Notre-Dame Cathedral (France)
Name: Paris, Banks of the Seine
Year: 1991

11 Westminster Abbey (United Kingdom)
Name: Westminster Palace, Westminster Abbey and Saint Margaret's Church
Year: 1987

12 Ironbridge (United Kingdom)
Name: Ironbridge Gorge
Year: 1986

13 Altes Museum, Museum Island, Berlin (Germany)
Name: Museumsinsel (Museum Island), Berlin
Year: 1999

14 Rila Monastery (Bulgaria)
Name: Rila Monastery
Year: 1983

15 Square of Zachariás Renaissance Houses (Czech Republic)
Name: Historic Centre of Telc
Year: 1992

16 Parthenon (Greece)
Name: Acropolis, Athens
Year: 1987

17 Meteora Monastery (Greece)
Name: Meteora
Year: 1988

18 Transfiguration Church on Kizhi Island (Russia)
Name: Kizhi Pogost
Year: 1990

19 Hagia Sofia (Turkey)
Name: Historic Areas of Istanbul
Year: 1985

20 Cappadocia Church (Turkey)
Name: Göreme National Park and the Rock Sites of Cappadocia
Year: 1985

21 Hatra (Iraq)
Name: Hatra
Year: 1985

22 Old Walled City of Shibam (Yemen)
Name: Old Walled City of Shibam
Year: 1982

23 Taj Mahal (India)
Name: Taj Mahal
Year: 1983

24 Angkor Wat (Cambodia)
Name: Angkor
Year: 1992

25 Borobudur (Indonesia)
Name: Borobudur Temple Compounds
Year: 1991

26 The Great Wall (China)
Name: The Great Wall
Year: 1987

27 Potala Palace (China)
Name: Historic Ensemble of the Potala Palace, Lhasa
Year: 1994, 2000, 2001

28 Changdeok Palace (Republic of Korea)
Name: Changdeokgung Palace Complex
Year: 1997

29 Chongmyo Shrine (Republic of Korea)
Name: Jongmyo Shrine
Year: 1995

30 Himeji Castle (Japan)
Name: Himeji-jo
Year: 1993

31 Kiyomizu Temple (Japan)
Name: Historic Monuments of Ancient Kyoto (Kyoto, Uji and Otsu Cities)
Year: 1994

32 Ginkakuji (Japan)
Name: Historic Monuments of Ancient Kyoto (Kyoto, Uji and Otsu Cities)
Year: 1994

33 Phoenix Hall of Byodo-in (Japan)
Name: Historic Monuments of Ancient Kyoto (Kyoto, Uji and Otsu Cities)
Year: 1994

34 Toji Five-storied Pagoda (Japan)
Name: Historic Monuments of Ancient Kyoto (Kyoto, Uji and Otsu Cities)
Year: 1994

35 Todaiji Great South Gate (Japan)
Name: Historic Monuments of Ancient Nara
Year: 1998

36 Historic Villages of Shirakawa-go and Gokayama (Japan)
Name: Historic Villages of Shirakawa-go and Gokayama
Year: 1995

37 Shuri Castle (Japan)
Name: Gusuku Sites and Related Properties of the Kingdom of Ryukyu
Year: 2000

38 Statue of Liberty (United States)
Name: Statue of Liberty
Year: 1984

39 Taos Pueblo (United States)
Name: Pueblo de Taos
Year: 1992

40 Pyramid of the Magician (Mexico)
Name: Pre-Hispanic Town of Uxmal
Year: 1996

41 Havana Cathedral (Cuba)
Name: Old Havana and its Fortifications
Year: 1982

42 San Nicolás de Bari Hospital (Dominican Republic)
Name: Colonial City of Santo Domingo
Year: 1990

43 Machu Picchu (Peru)
Name: Historic Sanctuary of Machu Picchu
Year: 1983

44 Moais (Chile)
Name: Rapa Nui National Park
Year: 1995

45 Congress Building, Brasilia (Brazil)
Name: Brasilia
Year: 1987

あとがき

　2005年春、沖縄の旅から帰って間もないとき、彰国社より今回のお話を頂きました。本のテーマは「世界遺産」。世界遺産となると折り紙の主体は建築物。どちらかといえば、これまでは花や動物など、建築物以外のものが多かった私にとっては、茶谷先生の作品にどこまで近づけるかという新たな挑戦となりました。ご存知のように、折り紙建築はケント紙のサイズを自ら規定し、その中でいかに立体を表現し、かつ畳めるかが真髄です。小さなケント紙の中に、世界遺産という巨大な遺跡や建物を埋め込む作業は、先生が口上で述べられているように、まさに「時空を旅すること限りなし」です。

　私の場合、建築物の立面や形態を折り紙化するとき、可能な限り細かく作る傾向にあるため、今回はかなり複雑な作品が多くなりました。そのため、これまでの折り紙建築の作り方では、ケント紙に写す穴印の数が多すぎて、型図を外した後の線種の判定が困難なため、本書の作り方にあるように、型図の上からカットする方法をとりました。また、これまで出版された折り紙建築の本では、90°タイプ以外の作品も紹介しておりましたが、本書では、作品の対象が世界遺産という、広く知られているものが多いだけに、180°のタイプでは形が単純化されすぎてイメージが伝わりにくいのではと考え、あえて90°タイプに限定させて頂きました。でも正直なところ、90°の作品はデザインが決まるまでが一番難しく、また表現が細かいほど折り上げるのも簡単ではありません。

　地球に優しくないのかも知れませんが、小さな屑籠はすぐに埋もれてしまいました。でも、それは折り紙建築の基本である90°タイプの奥の深さを、改めて認識できたことに対するご褒美だと思っています。

※

　私の作品製作にあたり協力してくださいました、兵頭喜代子さん・陸（くが）邦子さんに心より御礼申し上げます。また、建築の専門でない私に、助言や図面の作成等を援助してくれた、主人の中澤敏彰に感謝いたします。

中沢圭子

Postscript

Soon after my return from a trip to Okinawa, early in March 2005, Shokokusha contacted me about doing this book. Its concept: "World Heritage Sites." In bringing World Heritage sites to origami paper craft, our subject would be "buildings." My previous involvement, in this series, had mostly been in the design of flowers and animals—things other than buildings, so to see how closely I could approach Masahiro Chatani's origami works represented a new challenge for me.

The crux of designing Origamic Architecture is to choose, by one's own reckoning, a model size on Kent (construction) paper and figure out how to express a three-dimensional form within that size, as well as how to fold it. The work of fitting colossal World Heritage buildings or sites into small sheets of Kent paper, as Chatani mentions in his preface, is truly to travel "without limits through time and space."

Since I prefer a design that is as detailed as possible, when expressing through origami the facade or form of a building, this time you will find many models of complicated design. Because they are complicated, the method prescribed until now for making the models results in too many pinpricks when transferring the image to Kent paper, so that, after removing the pattern, it is difficult to distinguish the different lines. For the method prescribed in this book, therefore, we have adopted the technique of cutting the cutting line directly through the pattern.

Also, while previous Origamic Architecture books have included origami models of other types besides the 90°-angle type, we have chosen to present only the 90°-type in this book. Considering how widely known and recognized these World Heritage site buildings are, we felt that the form becomes too simplified with the 180°-type, so that the image is not rendered to satisfaction. Frankly, however, the process of designing each model proved to be the most difficult with the 90°-type. Because the image is rendered with so much detail, moreover, developing the folds was not an easy task either.

Because of that difficulty, my little wastebasket was soon filled to the top. While hardly an environmentally friendly turn of events, I saw it as evidence of my having freshly grasped the depth and sophistication of the 90°-type model, which is the foundation of Origamic Architecture.

I would like to express my heartfelt gratitude to Kiyoko Hyodo and Kuniko Kuga for their invaluable assistance during the design labors. As someone not specialized in architecture, I am also indebted to my husband, Toshiaki Nakazawa, for his advice and for his assistance with the designs and other aspects of this project.

Keiko Nakazawa

著者プロフィール　Authors：

茶谷正洋（ちゃたに　まさひろ）

1934年広島生まれ。1956年東京工業大学卒業。建設省（現国土交通省）建築研究所研究員、東京工業大学教授、静岡文化芸術大学教授、法政大学教授、東京工業大学名誉教授などを歴任。工学博士。2008年死去。
1981年に創始した折り紙建築の家元として一大ブームを呼び、展覧会、講師などで国内外に幅広く活躍。作り続けている折り紙建築の作品は2,000点以上にも及び、折り紙建築の著書も多数ある。

主な著書
〈折り紙建築〉シリーズ（彰国社）、『ポップアップカード』（雄鶏社）、『ペーパーマジックの世界』（雄鶏社）、『とびだすおりがみ』（ポプラ社）、『世界の建築まるごと事典』（日本実業出版社）その他多数

主な展覧会
1981年　銀座松屋にて折り紙建築展
2001年　ニューヨーク　アメリカン・クラフト・ミュージアムにて折り紙建築展
　　　　東京ガス横浜ショールームにて茶谷正洋のかみわざ展
2005年　折り紙建築サークル「風」講師
　　　　自由学園明日館にて茶谷正洋の折り紙建築展　その他多数

Masahiro CHATANI
1934: Born in Hiroshima. 1956: Graduated from Tokyo Institute of Technology. Posts have included Researcher, Architectural Research Institute, Ministry of Construction (present Ministry of Land, Infrastructure and Transport); Professor, Tokyo Institute of Technology; Professor, Shizuoka University of Art and Culture; and Professor, Hosei University; Professor Emeritus, Tokyo Institute of Technology Doctor of Engineering. It died in 2008.
Awakened popular interest in Origamic Architecture after originating this genre in 1981. Is widely active in Japan and abroad, holding exhibitions of his works, lecturing, etc. Has created over 2,000 Origamic Architecture works and authored numerous Origamic Architecture books.

Major Publications
Origamic Architecture Series (Shokokusha); *Pop-up Cards* (Ondorisha); *World of Paper Magic* (Ondorisha); *Pop-up Origami* (Popurasha); *Encyclopedia of Architecture* (Nihon Jitsugyo Shuppansha); and numerous others.

Major Exhibitions
1981: Origamic Architecture Exhibition, Ginza Matsuya
2001: Origamic Architecture Exhibition, New York American Craft Museum; Masahiro Chatani Kamiwaza Exhibition, Tokyo Gas Yokohama Showroom
2005: Lecturer, Origamic Architecture Circle "Kaze"; Masahiro Chatani Origamic Architecture Exhibition, Jiyugakuen Myonichikan; and numerous others.

中沢圭子（なかざわ　けいこ）

名古屋生まれ。1983年より折り紙建築を始める。
現在、折り紙建築アトリエブーケ主宰、紙ニュケーションアート・開主宰。
また、朝日カルチャー・西武コミュニティカレッジ・NHK文化センター・東急セミナーほか、多数の講師を務める。
花や動物などを題材にデザインされた作品はその華やかさ、かわいらしさが多くの人に親しまれている。最近はグリーティングカードの枠を超えてインテリア、アートとしての作品も多く手掛ける。今回は世界遺産という本格的な建築のジャンルに挑戦。
単行本、講師、展覧会など、めまぐるしい毎日を送る。

主な著書
『ホワイトクリスマス』（共著、講談社）、『折り紙建築　花鳥の巻』（共著、彰国社）
『折り紙建築　四季折々のカードをつくる』（彰国社）、『折り紙建築　グリーティングカード集』（彰国社）、『楽しく作れるグリーティングカード』（雄鶏社）、『立体グリーティングカード』（ブティック社）
『切りあそび、紙あそび』（日本文芸社）その他多数

主な展覧会
1988年　西武百貨店池袋アトリエヌーボーにて折り紙建築百華展
1990年　いわさきちひろ美術館企画展にてORIGAMIC MAGICAL ZONE
1997年　銀座伊東屋にて紙のポエム展
2001年　ニューヨーク　アメリカン・クラフト・ミュージアムにて折り紙建築展
2002年　銀座伊東屋にて中沢圭子のペーパーアート KAI 真夏の和楽展　その他多数

Keiko NAKAZAWA
Born in Nagoya. 1983: Began to create Origamic Architecture.
Currently is President, Origamic Architecture Atelier Bouquet; and President, Kaminication Art KAI. Also lectures at Asahi Culture, Seibu Community College, NHK Bunka Center, Tokyu Seminar, etc.
Her works depicting flowers and animals are widely known for their cute, elaborately rendered design. Has recently transcended the greeting card field to create numerous origami interior decorative works and art works. In undertaking World Heritage sites, this time, she brings her talents to a purely architectural genre.
Pursues a hectic daily schedule of book writing, lectures, and exhibitions.

Major Publications
White Christmas (co-author, Kodansha); *A Paradise of Origamic Architecture* (co-author, Shokokusha); *Origamic Architecture Greeting Cards for the Four Seasons* (Shokokusha); *Origamic Architecture Greeting Cards* (Shokokusha); *Greeting Cards Fun to Make* (Ondorisha); *3D Pop-up Greeting Cards* (Boutique-sha); *Origamic Architecture Greeting Cards* (Nihonbungeisha) and numerous others.

Major Exhibitions
1988: Origamic Architecture Exhibition, Atelier Nouveau, Seibu Department Store, Ikebukuro
1990: Origamic Magical Zone, Chihiro Art Museum
1997: Paper Poem Exhibition, Ginza Itoya
2001: Origamic Architecture Exhibition, New York American Craft Museum
2002: Keiko Nakazawa Paper Art KAI Midsummer Waraku Exhibition, Ginza Itoya; and numerous others.

折り紙建築　世界遺産をつくろう！
2005年11月20日　第1版　発　行
2012年 6月10日　第1版　第6刷

	著　者	茶 谷 正 洋・中 沢 圭 子
著作権者との協定により検印省略	発行者	後　藤　　　武
	発行所	株式会社　彰　国　社

自然科学書協会会員
工 学 書 協 会 会 員

162-0067　東京都新宿区富久町8-21
電話　03-3359-3231(大代表)
振替口座　00160-2-173401

Printed in Japan

ⓒ　茶谷正洋・中沢圭子　2005年　　　製版・印刷：壮光舎印刷　製本：中尾製本
ISBN 4-395-27047-6 C 3072　　　http://www.shokokusha.co.jp

本書の内容の一部あるいは全部を、無断で複写（コピー）、複製、および磁気または光記録媒体等への入力を禁止します。許諾については小社あてご照会ください。